A HARD FOUGHT BATTLE

For six days and nights, Linda fought for the woman's life. On the seventh day, as she approached the bed with steaming poultices which she had just soaked in hot water, the sick woman turned her head on the pillow.

"Leave me alone," she whispered, "I can't struggle any more."

Linda found herself speaking almost in anger. "What do you mean," she demanded, "by giving up? You have a family. Your children need you!" And she continued to apply the hot poultices, determined to go on until the woman either died or revived. An hour passed—an hour of grim, gasping struggle.

Then suddenly the woman's breathing became more normal. The blue-choked look left her face. Her temperature dropped. A light perspiration broke out on her forehead.

When Dr. Dimock came, she said to Linda, "The crisis has passed. You have done what a nurse can sometimes do—even better than a doctor. You have saved this woman's life!"

AMERICA'S FIRST TRAINED NURSE:
Linda Richards
was originally published by Julian Messner.

Critics' Corner:

"For girls...who are considering nursing careers this is an inspiring and serious biography which presents a vivid picture of the early days of nurses' training here and in England. Recommended."
—Library Journal

"...a tremendously moving story of a young Vermont farm girl who from childhood wanted to care for the sick.... As a warm and personal account of a dedicated woman, the story of Linda Richards should be both popular and inspiring."
—Elementary English

"It is an incredible list of accomplishments for one person, each of them made in the face of formidable opposition and ignorance. Girls brought up on *Sue Barton* will be amazed and sobered, but also inspired and grateful." *—Horn Book*

Other Recommendations: Child Study Association, H. W. Wilson Junior High School Library Catalog.

About the Author:

RACHEL BAKER grew up in the little town of Dickinson, North Dakota, and went to the University of Minnesota. After a two-year stay in Europe, she returned to the United States, got married, had two children, and began her writing career. She has been a journalist, a feature writer, and a contributor of medical articles for a national syndicate. She is now one of the leading biographers in the teen-age field, and also finds time to be a teacher and lecturer. Among her many popular books for young people is *The First Woman Doctor: The Story of Elizabeth Blackwell, M.D.*

AMERICA'S FIRST TRAINED NURSE LINDA RICHARDS

Born: July 27, 1841
Died: April 16, 1930

———◆———

by Rachel Baker

AN ARCHWAY PAPERBACK
WASHINGTON SQUARE PRESS • NEW YORK

AMERICA'S FIRST TRAINED NURSE:
Linda Richards

Archway Paperback edition published February, 1970

2nd printing....................October, 1970

                                                              L
Published by Washington Square Press,
a division of Simon & Schuster, Inc., 630 Fifth Avenue, New York, N.Y.

Acknowledgment

With Gratitude—

Many people make a book possible. My husband, Joseph Baker, and my daughter, Joanna Baker Merlen, helped greatly. My editor, Gertrude Blumenthal, has always helped.

I am grateful to the Boston City Hospital, the Massachusetts General Hospital, and to the New England Hospital for Women and Children for their help.

I am particularly indebted to Miss Katherine Berry and to her publishers, the Fleming H. Revell Company, for permission to quote in chapters 14 and 15 of my book, from Miss Berry's biography of her father, *A Pioneer Doctor in Old Japan.* The material in the language lesson in my book, pages 148-151, is based on information in Miss Berry's book, and also on such material first cited in *Thirty Eventful Years,* by M. L. Gordon.

Miss Berry answered my many questions about

Acknowledgment

Miss Richards' life in Japan, most patiently. In addition, I received from Miss Berry copies of letters, original letters, and a catalogue of Doshisha University in Japan, published at the time of Linda Richards' work there.

I would like to acknowledge also the help of the American Journal of Nursing.

R. B.

To Connie, Monty and Mary-Ellen

AMERICA'S
FIRST TRAINED
NURSE
LINDA RICHARDS

Chapter I

The snow had lain frozen all winter long on the hills of Vermont. Folks gathering in the village store in Newport to watch the weekly coach go by said they had never seen such a winter.

The village, comprising no more than a shoe-string of houses, lay at the edge of frozen Lake Memphremagog, thirty miles long, stretching like a sea of the Arctic into Canada.

When school let out for the day in the little one-room schoolhouse near the rim of the lake, all the children but one ran down to the Narrows, an inlet kept clear in winter for skating.

As this child, a dark-eyed girl of ten, was about to leave the schoolroom, the teacher, a graying spinster, spoke to her kindly.

"How is your mother feeling, Linda?" she asked.

The girl shook her head with a worried look. "She coughs all the time and she doesn't eat a thing. She hasn't been out of her bed once this winter!"

"That's the way it is with consumption," the teacher remarked in the plain way of the New England people, who speak always without being squeamish, in a manner which to others might seem brusque.

"But still," she went on, "when the weather gets warm and the sun comes out, then your mother may feel better again."

The girl glanced toward the window where there still hung, late in March, the long gray icicles which had not melted all winter.

She left the schoolhouse carrying the serge bag into which she had stuffed her books and her tin lunch box. She was a rather large-boned girl for her age, with wide shoulders and a firm chin. She had about her the look of a child who has never learned to play, who has always carried adult worries.

She took a road which led past the town and away from the Narrows, from which there could be heard through the high bare trees, the sound of the other schoolchildren laughing and shouting as they sped gaily over the ice.

Soon the village and the lake disappeared behind her as she climbed one snowy hill and then another. Finally she turned in at a little gray farmhouse from which a thin spiral of smoke showed in the cold, clear air.

She went around to the back of the house and lifted the latch of the door with numbed fingers. A large striped cat rose from the braided rug by the kitchen stove and greeted her with a hungry meow.

"Hush, pussy!" she warned.

Linda hung up her wraps and put away her books. Then moving just as quietly as she could in her copper-toed boots, she poked up the fire and put on the tea kettle to boil. As she worked she kept listening.

Once a week, her sisters went down to the village, carrying a bucket of butter they had churned. They left the house before Linda came home from school in order to reach the store before the weekly coach left for Boston, loaded with produce.

Linda warmed her hands by the stove. She never went into her mother's room bringing the chill of the outside air with her. From the room beyond she heard the sound of coughing, and then a faint voice called, "Is that you, Linda?" Although christened Melinda Ann, she was all her life to be known by her nickname of Linda.

"Coming, Mother!"

She crossed the dining room where a hymnbook stood open on the melodeon, and above it there hung the picture of a sad young man, his face framed by a dusty wreath of pressed flowers.

On a huge wooden bed in a little alcove of the dining room which was heated by a pot-bellied stove, a sick woman lay propped high on pillows. Her fallen temples and hollow cheeks made her dark eyes look too large for her face. She turned them toward Linda with a dazed and feverish look.

Linda smoothed out the pillows. "How do you feel, Mother?" she asked, sinking down at the bedside, gently stroking her mother's thin hand.

The sick woman wrinkled her forehead, staring at the window where the icicles hung glittering in the last yellow rays of the sun. She said in an odd, faraway voice, "I keep dozing and dreaming."

"What do you dream about, Mother?"

"I thought we were back in Wisconsin," she said, wetting her lips with effort, "in that cabin in the woods where your father died."

The girl did not answer, and trying not to look upset she tucked the covers round her mother's thin shoulders. Her mother seemed to doze. Linda went out into the kitchen to start supper for her sisters.

It was five years since Linda's father had passed away in a cabin in the newly opened Wisconsin territory to which he had just brought his family.

They had come from a farm near Potsdam, New York, where Melinda Ann Judson, the youngest of the Richards children had been born, July 27, 1841, just as the first news came of the settlement of the Black Hawk War and the opening of the Wisconsin territory.

Many families left their farms in upper New York State to settle in the Wisconsin wilderness, where huge tracts of rich farmland were available.

When Linda was five years old, her family moved to Wisconsin, to a tract of land near the tumbling Rock River, where the city of Watertown now stands.

There Linda's father felled the tall trees and built a cabin in an area of pinewoods which he had been told would be good for his health, for he had long suffered from an affliction of the lungs.

Only a few weeks after the cabin was finished, he died suddenly of a hemorrhage of the lungs, and his widow with her three small children returned to her girlhood home in Vermont.

There Mrs. Richards bought a farm, not far from her father's farm, near Newport, and very soon she showed signs of the same illness which had taken the life of her husband.

She coughed, she ate very little, she grew thin and feverish. During the summers she rallied. In the winters she often lay ill in bed for months at a time. The last winter she had not risen at all.

Old Dr. Currier, who came up from the village flushed and puffing, no longer brought bottles of brown mixture for the sick woman. Shaking his head dubiously, he said, repeatedly, "We can only hope for spring."

Although Linda was the youngest, she seemed to be best at nursing her mother. Laura, the eldest, a thin, sallow girl of fifteen, silent, abrupt in her movements, had no hand with the sick. Her mother always begged, "Why don't you wait and let Linda do it for me when she comes?"

Elizabeth, who was thirteen, a softly rounded girl with blonde hair as fine as a baby's, and big blue eyes that filled with tears too easily, always upset her mother by crying.

Linda knew by instinct just how to fix a tray prettily, how to turn over a pillow, how to make the sheets smooth. And as if she had been born with the ability to see more than others, she sensed the most minute changes in her mother's condition.

She had amazed Dr. Currier one day by telling him that every afternoon her mother's cheeks grew flushed, that her eyes looked too bright.

"I believe she is feverish."

He shook his head. "If you were a boy I would say that you would make a very fine doctor."

"I should never want to be a doctor," Linda replied, firmly objecting.

"What then?" He puffed out his fat cheeks.

"I will take care of sick people. Somebody has to nurse them, and I will be the one to do it!"

When this remark was repeated to Grandpa Sinclair, the tall, grave old gentleman stroked his white side whiskers and shook his head in an odd way. "What else has the child known all her life but sickness?"

The endless winter continued week after week, with snow and sleet, and with icy winds sweeping from Canada over frozen 'Magog.

Every day after school, Linda ran home to sit

6

beside her mother. She made milk toast with cinnamon and nutmeg.

"Doesn't that smell nice?" she coaxed. "Won't you take a little?"

She brought in a tumbler of fragrant beef tea, "Just take one sip, Mother, a little sip to please me."

She cajoled and coaxed. At night she rose to listen to her mother's breathing. Her sister Laura slept on a cot in the kitchen. But it was Linda, sleeping in a little cold room beyond, who always seemed to sense when her mother awakened.

"Is it still the middle of the night?" her mother sometimes asked, when Linda, hearing her mother stirring, came in on tiptoe with hot tea or warm milk.

"No, it's not the middle of the night," Linda said, sitting down by the bed and taking her mother's hand gently, "It's the middle of summer. And you and I are sitting on the porch, under the wisteria bush. The birds are singing, and the bees are humming. . . . "

She put her cheek against her mother's hand and kept on talking in a dreamy voice about the wonders of midsummer, until she knew by her mother's breathing that she had fallen asleep.

Toward the middle of April there came at last the long-delayed "March" thaw. Rills ran from the hills. The children leaped joyously over icy puddles.

Linda came running home with something treasured in her hand. It was a tiny blade of green grass. "Look Mother, I found it growing at the edge of the snow!"

But spring came too late for the sick woman. On a night when the booming wind swept the last of the snow from the hills, the three girls watching by their mother's bedside saw her sink into her final sleep.

The little gray farmhouse was sold; the melodeon and the picture of Linda's father, framed with pressed flowers, were packed away in Grandpa Sinclair's attic.

It was arranged that Laura should go to live with a distant relative in Boston, and Linda and Elizabeth were to stay with Grandpa Sinclair and his second wife, a stout, toothless old woman, who sat all day long vaguely making patchwork quilts.

On a June morning, when the furniture had been taken away and all the packing cases had gone to be stored in Grandpa's attic, Linda went from window to window, in the empty farmhouse where she had taken care of her mother.

Outside the cart waited with the last of the family belongings. Elizabeth, and also Laura, who was to stay at her grandfather's for a few days before she went to Boston, waited in the cart.

Laura called impatiently. "Why are you poking around in that empty house? Aren't you ever coming?"

"Right away!" Linda answered.

Linda Richards

She came out on the porch. The wisteria vine hung over the porch drooping with heavy purple blossoms. At her mother's funeral Linda had not cried. People had looked at her as if wondering if she had any feelings.

Now, looking up at the purple blossoms which her mother had longed to see, Linda found herself sobbing. The tears ran down her cheeks. She rubbed them away with the back of her hand.

Then drawing a deep breath, she went down the path in her black dress, which was too long for her and which flapped at her heels.

"I can't imagine," said Laura, as she took up the reins with a frown, "what kept you so long."

Linda did not answer. She climbed into the cart and took her place beside her sisters. Her lips quivered slightly. Then the wheels began to turn, and the cart, bearing the three girls sitting erect in their black dresses, passed slowly down the long dusty road.

Chapter II

A few weeks later, on his way to see a patient, Dr. Currier stopped one morning for a few moments at the Sinclair farm.

"Where is Linda?" he asked.

Old Mrs. Sinclair, dozing on the porch over a basket of quilt pieces, lifted her toothless face and pointed vaguely toward the back of the house.

Dr. Currier went around to the kitchen door, where he found Linda in the buttery scrubbing the last of the milkpans.

"Dr. Currier," she gasped.

She followed him into the yard, where he sat down on the well curb, and breathing heavily, mopped his round red face. He surveyed her from under puffy eyelids.

"Look at you," he scolded. "Your shoulders stick out like chicken wings. And if your chin gets any sharper, you might well use it to cut bread and spread butter."

She looked down and traced a circle in the dust

with her bare toe. "I feel useless," she said disconsolately."I have nobody to tend!"

He rose with a sigh. "Child, child, if you only knew how many sick and suffering things there are in this world that need tending."

Sometime later, toward the end of summer, he once more passed the sagging old farmhouse with age-darkened shutters which looked out gloomily on the road.

He discovered Elizabeth, her golden hair in curl-papers, sitting at the kitchen door shelling peas for dinner. He asked for Linda.

Elizabeth wrinkled her nose. "She's down in the barn with her froggery."

"Froggery?"

He went out to the big, shadowy barn smelling of horses, harness and hay. He found Linda kneeling over a dishpan of water. On a rock placed in the center of the dishpan sat a frog.

The frog did not move. Tied to one of his legs was a roughly made splint, padded with a bit of rag which had grayed evidently from soaking in the water.

"What do you have there?"

The doctor squatted, puffing, his chin and his paunch almost meeting. Linda hastened to give him a stool so he could sit down more comfortably.

"It's a sick frog," she said. "His leg was broken."

"I see," said the doctor studying the patient who

blinked at him by pulling up his lower lid much as you might pull up a stocking.

Linda went to get the frog a dead fly, which he gulped up appreciatively. Then kneeling in the straw she told the doctor how she and her sister had found the frog, near the pond at the end of the cow pasture, sitting helplessly on a rock.

"Some boys must have stoned him," she said indignantly. "There he was, with his leg bruised, unable to move. I knew if I didn't help him a snake would get him."

"Sure enough bait," said the doctor listening seriously. "How did you get the hurt frog home?"

"In my sunbonnet," replied Linda watching the frog who goggled at her, his throat pulsating as if he were waiting for another fly.

"I scooped up some wet ferns in my sunbonnet, and then I carried the frog home in his own little cool litter."

"I daresay your sister didn't help you."

"Oh, she called him a nasty old thing, and she wouldn't touch him or go near him. You know some people don't like frogs. But he's really no different from any other living thing."

"Of course not."

"At first I thought his leg would get better, if I just kept him safe here in the barn and fed him well."

"Often a prime treatment," remarked the doctor.

"I made this froggery as you see. I kept the water fresh. And I put this rock in the center, so that if the frog wanted to he could sit where it was dry.

"But pretty soon," Linda went on, and she took out from her pocket another dead fly, "I saw that his leg would never get better unless it was set."

"Hm-m," said the doctor, scratching his nose and looking down thoughtfully as the frog gobbled up another fly. "How did you proceed?"

"I took a smooth little stick and I padded it by winding a piece of lint around it. I thought that the stick next to the frog's poor leg surely would hurt him."

"Naturally."

"Then I very gently felt the leg. Even through the swelling, I could feel a little place where it seemed to me the bone was broken."

"Quite so," said the doctor.

"Well, I shut my eyes and then, holding the frog between my knees I pushed the two parts of the bone together. It must have hurt him terribly, because he gave a dreadful jerk. And my heart jerked, too!"

"I know exactly how you felt," said the doctor gravely.

She nodded. "But there was nothing to do but finish. So I held the broken leg against the splint, and I tied it securely into place.

"Afterward," she confided, "I worried. I thought

maybe I had put on the splint too tightly. I kept going out to the barn to look at the frog. I couldn't tell by the color of his toes—or even by the feel—whether I had hurt his leg by bandaging it so tightly."

"And you couldn't ask the patient?" said Dr. Currier, his expression serious. But in his eye there was a slight twinkle.

Linda smiled, reached into her pocket and took out one more dead fly. She dropped it—and with an almost imperceptible lunge, the frog gulped it down.

"He likes flies and all other kinds of insects. He prefers them freshly caught. His appetite is quite good, and feeding him has kept me very busy."

"Indeed," said the doctor. "And when were you thinking of taking off the splint?"

"Well, he's been pretty nimble the last few days, hopping round with the splint in the funniest way. But I have no way of knowing, really, whether it's time to take off the splint."

"H-mm." Dr. Currier reached into his pocket and took out a small penknife which he used for paring his nails. "With your permission, I could make an examination."

"Oh please do!" Kneeling, Linda held the frog for a moment, saying softly, "There, there, this won't hurt you."

Dr. Currier with a deft touch cut the bandage which was tied around the splint, and unwinding the rag which held the padded piece of wood, he gently felt the frog's leg.

"No swelling," he commented, "no sign of inflammation or tenderness. It might feel stiff for a moment or two, but I daresay he'll soon be hopping on that leg."

"Do I have to let him go?"

"He'll be happier in the pond."

"Whom will I tend now?" she said disconsolately.

Linda did not see Dr. Currier again until well along in the haying season, when he came by one day in a great hurry. He didn't even get out of the buggy.

"I need someone to help me," he told Linda who had come running out to greet him. She still looked thin, but she was not as pale as she had been before.

He told Linda that he was on his way to a farmer who had fallen off a hayrack the week before, and who lay sick with fever. And, on another farm, a woman who had been sitting up all night long with her baby, needed someone to relieve her.

"That poor woman is all tuckered out."

"Who should go?"

"Well, I thought you took care of the frog pretty well."

Linda raced to the kitchen, her dark hair flying. "Elizabeth," she cried, "I'm going with Dr. Currier to nurse a sick baby."

15

"What?" Elizabeth was cutting out a dress from a newspaper pattern pinned to a piece of gingham, and she dropped the scissors to stare.

"When will you be back?"

"When the baby is better!"

Linda, jogging in the buggy beside the doctor, listened intently to his directions. The baby was having convulsions, he told her.

"What do they come from?"

"Usually from letting the baby eat something he shouldn't, like sometimes the mother will let the baby suck on a bit of fat meat."

"What happens?"

Dr. Currier carefully described the symptoms: the sharp cry, the way the baby would draw up its legs, throw back its head, arch its body and stiffen out like a turned-over canoe.

"What will I do?"

"Put the baby in a warm mustard bath. Be sure to use very little mustard. A baby's skin is tender. Test the water with your elbow to be sure it's not too warm."

"How long do I bathe him?"

"Until his cheeks get pink and his limbs relax, and he stretches and yawns. Then dry him and put him to bed."

"Is that all?"

"No. Each time the baby has a convulsion, you do the same thing."

"You mean over and over again?"

"Yes, that's why the baby's mother is so tired."

"I can help her," said Linda firmly.

Dr. Currier let Linda off at a little brown farmhouse. The kitchen door stood open. Inside a woman lay against the table, her head sprawled on her arms.

She looked at Linda dazed, her dark thin hair in disarray, deep circles around her eyes. "Did Dr. Currier send somebody to help me?" she asked.

"Yes," Linda replied.

"Where's the woman?"

"He sent me."

"But you're only a child," she shook her head in dismay. "I'm all worn out," she wailed, "I need somebody that knows what they're doing."

"Sit there for a minute," Linda gently suggested, "while I poke up the fire and bring in some water for the wash boiler. I see it's almost empty."

The woman gave a moan. "I knew I'd be needin' water, but I just didn't have the strength to go for it. I felt if that baby cried again, I just couldn't get up once more to tend him."

She slumped forward on the table, shut her eyes for a moment and almost instantly fell asleep. In a corner of the kitchen stood a crib in which a baby turned restlessly, the bluish eyelids fluttering now and then, the tiny hands clenching.

Linda put wood on the stove. From the well she brought in first one pail of water and then another. She poured water into the wash boiler which stood on the stove, being careful not to splash or make a sound.

She found the baby's tin tub, and put in a folded cloth to make it soft. She measured out the exact amount of mustard as the doctor had directed. She prepared a light cotton blanket.

The woman slept. The baby slept, too, but ever more restlessly, twisting and turning, moaning sometimes. Then suddenly the baby let out a scream.

"There he goes!" the woman sprang up.

Instantly, Linda prepared the bath, her heart racing, the baby's cry echoing again and again, boring into her ears.

"Do something!" screamed the woman.

Linda remembered to test the water with her elbow. The baby's eyes rolled back, his face turned blue, his body arched and stiffened.

Linda took the stark baby in her arms, and supporting the back of his head with her palm, lowered him carefully into the warm mustard bath.

"There, there," she soothed, "you're going to feel better soon." The mother wrung her hands.

"He'll die!" she cried. "He'll die!"

Convulsion after convulsion ran through the baby's body. But at length the warm water seemed to soothe him. The twitching stopped.

Laving the warm water over him with her other hand, Linda could feel his body relaxing. He stretched, gave a yawn and opened his eyes.

"You poor little thing," she murmured, "you've had a bad time."

The mother moaned with relief. Linda dried the baby by patting him gently with the blanket, all the time talking soothingly to him.

He was a thin baby, perhaps not yet a year old. His face looked exhausted and old, and his ribs showed from the rigor of the convulsions which had come and gone for almost forty-eight hours.

Linda put the baby to bed. Then she emptied the tin tub, hung out the blanket to dry and added more water to the boiler on the stove.

She persuaded Mrs. Brewster, the mother, to go into the bedroom to lie down. "I will call you," Linda told her, "if you are needed. Let me watch now, while you sleep a little."

The woman stumbled out wearily. "I shouldn't leave him, but I'll sleep only a minute or two. My head is spinning so that I don't know what I'm doing."

All afternoon she slept. Time after time, Linda bathed the sick baby when he woke screaming, his body twitching with convulsions.

Time after time she lowered him into the soothing bath, wondering as he gasped and his body rose rigid, if he were going to die, if she should have called his mother.

But each time the tremor passed, each time the baby went limp in her arms, then relaxed with a deep sigh as the faint color came back to the pinched cheeks.

Finally he slept quietly in his crib. Linda tidied the kitchen and made a cup of tea. Then she went into the bedroom to call the mother.

The tired woman came out into the kitchen dazed. She looked around, her hand on her heart, her eyes frightened. "I thought the baby was worse!"

"No, no," Linda whispered. "He's been sleeping quite peacefully for over an hour."

The weary woman sat down and drank her tea and ate the bread and butter which Linda set out for her. When she had finished she looked up, her eyes brimming with tears of gratitude.

"You're a born nurse," she said.

After that, when children became sick with the croup, with coughs or measles, when babies had convulsions, the exhausted mothers said, "Send a cart for that Richards girl."

The next few years passed. Linda grew into a tall, dark-eyed girl, calm of manner, who went whenever she was called to help at a bed of sickness.

Chapter III

When Linda was sixteen years old she came home one night, just as the first light of morning began to show over the darkened fields.

For two weeks she had been nursing an old man, who lay sick and alone in a lonely farmhouse. All last night she had watched, and finally toward morning he had whispered, "I want to go home," and his head slipped down upon the pillow with the motion of a child who falls asleep.

She turned down the lamp a little, then went into the kitchen and put a lantern in the window to signal the neighbors, who had promised to come to watch the body.

After a time they came, a gnarled farmer and his son, swinging lanterns, their jaws unshaven, their eyes bleary, for neither had slept well, waiting for the signal.

"We'll sit now," said the father. The son grunted, this was his only greeting.

"I've made a pot of tea for you," Linda told

21

them, "and I've put out some bread and butter and jam on the table."

She went out, softly closing the door after her, just as she had moved softly in the house while she waited for those who were to sit with the dead.

As she walked home a gray light rose in the sky, and from the fields, looking black in this light, there rose a mist like a ghostly emanation.

She wondered about life and dying. What most people feared, she no longer feared. Dying was natural, and in its own way a part of life.

Yet the moment of death always awed her. For an instant she felt all the hopes, all the longings of the dying person, and it made her heart ache unbearably.

She let herself into her grandfather's darkened house. The kitchen had a damp, musty smell. She felt weary but knew she could not sleep.

She found a little pile of kindling by the stove. Her grandfather had evidently not expected her back so soon, and had planned to get up and start the fire and cook his own breakfast.

Linda and her grandfather lived alone now. Old Mrs. Sinclair had passed away. Linda's sister Elizabeth had married and moved with her husband to Providence, Rhode Island. Gradually both of Linda's sisters passed out of her life. She was rarely to hear from them.

Linda piled the shavings and kindling into the stove and lit the fire. The shavings began to crackle. She put on the kettle. The early morning light gradually filled the room.

Her grandfather appeared in the doorway in his stocking feet, his galluses dragging, his undershirt unbuttoned, and on his thin, unshaven face a startled look.

"So you're back?"

"Here, Grandpa, let me get you some tea."

She filled an earthenware cup with the dark, steaming liquid. She hurried to cut bread for him, spreading it thickly with homemade jam.

He drank with loud, appreciative gulps. She saw with a tug how glad he was to have her home again. She had been gone longer this time than ever before.

He lifted shaggy eyebrows. "Did the old man die?"

"Yes, just before it got light."

He took another loud sip. Almost all his teeth were gone, and in his old age he had become less meticulous, more noisy when he ate.

His brows moved again. "I wondered how it would be for you, all alone with someone who was dying?" He scratched his chest where a few gray hairs showed, and for a moment studied her.

She felt touched by his concern. "I thought I would be afraid," she admitted, "but I wasn't. When a person's been suffering, it's good to know that he won't suffer any more."

She rose to clear the table. He got up, and pulled his galluses with a twang over his bony shoulders.

23

Then he leaned down and began to pull on his boots, grunting because his feet, twisted with rheumatism, hurt him.

"I'll go, too, someday," he began, his face gray from the ordeal. "And when I do, I'll want to know that in some way you've been provided for."

"Please don't talk so, Grandpa. You're much more able than most men of your age, and you're going to live a long time."

"I spoke of this before, and I'm going to speak of it again. If you don't marry, you won't be able to run the farm. I want you to have a way to earn a living."

"But Grandpa, I can't leave you and go away to school. I wouldn't have gone this time if there had been anyone else able to take care of that poor dying man. I've only been gone two weeks—and look at you. You've probably not had a good meal since I left."

"I can fend for myself much better than you think. I've made up my mind, Linda, I want you to go to the Academy in St. Johnsbury and learn to be a teacher."

"But Grandpa, I'll never be good as a teacher. I have no calling for that work. I'm happiest when I can go out to take care of somebody that's sick, somebody that needs me, like that old man. There wasn't anybody to sit with him when he was dying."

"I know you're very apt at taking care of sick

people. But that's what you do for a neighbor. You couldn't take pay for it."

"No, of course not," she admitted.

"Then how are you going to earn a living?"

She had no answer but rose and began to wash the dishes. He hobbled out to start the day's work on the farm.

One evening several days later, as they sat reading the Boston newspapers, which came in once a week at the village post office, the topic came up again in an accidental way.

Grandpa, spelling out an editorial, grumbled about the election of Buchanan, who surely was going to bring the country into a worse panic than the one of 1837.

"Somehow these panics come every twenty years. Each time there's a reason. First we built too many canals. Now we've been building too many railroads."

He crackled the page, looking over his iron-rimmed glasses at the lamplight. As usual they sat in the kitchen. He went on indignantly, "Imagine wanting to reach California with a railroad. This panic of '57 is going to be the worse one we ever had."

Linda was poring over the inside pages of the paper, scarcely hearing a word. Suddenly she burst out, "The people of England are raising a fund to honor her."

"Honor whom?"

"The lady with the lamp!"

"Whatever are you talking about?"

"Florence Nightingale!"

"Who?" he put down his paper.

"Grandpa, Grandpa!" she cried. "I've told you a-bout her ever so many times. Now don't pretend that you've never heard about Florence Nightingale. The whole world knows what she has done."

"Oh, you mean that Englishwoman that went out to the Crimea and took care of some sick soldiers."

"Took care of some sick soldiers!" Linda exclaimed, her voice fervent, her cheeks glowing with excitement. "Do you know that she went out to the army barracks hospital at Scutari with only thirty-seven women, and organized the nursing of ten thousand sick and wounded men?

"They call her the lady with the lamp because she walked through the wards at night with her lamp, stopping at every bed, never going to sleep herself until she had looked after each and every sick and dying man.

"When she grew sick with fever, they say the soldiers in the hospital cried like babies. They called her their 'cheering angel.'

"Then when she recovered, and the British sent a man-of-war to take her home with great honor, do you know what she did? She slipped away and went home on a private vessel. She's a great woman. She doesn't care in the least about honors."

Linda leaned across the table. "But the people

of England did want to honor her. So they raised a great fund to give her as a gift. They call it the Florence Nightingale fund.

"And do you know what she is going to do with it? She is going to give it to a hospital in London, to start a school to train nurses."

"Now how can you train nurses?" Grandpa asked, regarding Linda in her enthusiasm with a rather troubled look. "If a woman is kindly then she can take care of someone that's sick."

"Oh, no, Grandpa. If you only knew how many times I wished I had somebody to teach me. Dr. Currier was kind and he used to take the trouble to tell me a little.

"But that new doctor, he just says all you need to know is how to put on a poultice. Yet many times when I was tending somebody that was sick, I wondered if I really was doing the right thing, and if there wasn't some better way to help them."

She put her cheek on her palm and looked into the yellow light of the flickering lamp. "If I were rich, if I could go to England, I would study to be a nurse."

"Now Melinda Ann Judson Richards," her grandfather used her full given name, which he never did except when he was about to lecture her. "Just you stop dreaming. You'll never get to England. How could such a ridiculous thing ever happen. As for studying to be a nurse, now you

27

had better put your head to quite another matter.

"I've made up my mind," he told her firmly. "With what I have left of my savings, you're going to be sent to the Academy in St. Johnsbury, to be educated as a teacher."

"But I have no call," she wailed.

"Every person has a call to provide for himself. And if you don't have the sense to plan your future, then I will.

"Until you marry, you can make your living by teaching in one of the village schools. When you're settled and have your own family, if you have any time hanging on your hands, then I'm sure your husband won't prevent you from going out to help a sick neighbor."

He looked at her sternly. "You're young and I'm old. I've seen a good deal more living than you have. Being a heroine is good enough for those that can afford it.

"But for you and me, just barely able to earn our bread and butter on this worn-out farm, why it's better for us to come to our senses. Now you just stop dreaming about ladies with lamps."

"Oh, Grandpa!"

The next morning Grandpa shaved, cutting himself several times. Then holding his head high with rasped dignity, he let her tie on his Sunday stock. He looked injured, as if getting into his Sunday clothes were somehow her fault.

Together they drove to the town of St. Johnsbury, some thirty miles away, where he enrolled Linda for the year of schooling which would enable her to become a teacher.

Chapter IV

"If it would not trouble you too much, Miss Richards," the Latin mistress said in an icy tone, "and if it would not divert you too greatly from your own interesting preoccupations, then may I request you please to decline for me the Latin verb *to love!*"

Linda had been studying the map in the geography book which lay open on top of her Latin grammar. She looked up startled.

"I'm not prepared."

"Not prepared?"

The Latin teacher, a tall, angular woman with a hawklike nose and a tight, bitter mouth, drew herself up like a bird of prey.

"Might I ask, Miss Richards," she said in a tone of pretended sweetness, and an appreciative titter ran through the schoolroom, "just what book you are so assiduously studying when you should be paying some slight attention to your Latin declensions?"

"It's a geography book," replied Linda, not

looking up, her heart thudding and her face flushing hotly.

"And why a geography book?" exclaimed the teacher in a baiting voice. "You know very well that we teach no such subject in the upper classes at the Academy."

"I was looking up something on the map."

"I suppose you would not hesitate to confide in us what you found it so necessary to look up, since the matter seemed to be of such significance that you paid no attention to the Latin class."

"I was trying to find the city of Scutari, which I thought lay in the Crimea, but I found out it was situated not far from Constantinople on the Bosporus."

"Edifying! Edifying, indeed!" cried the teacher with mocking enthusiasm. "Would we be intruding to ask why this place should be of such importance to you?"

Linda made no reply.

"Undoubtedly you do not plan an immediate journey to Scutari, so your preparations in tracing the route might be considered rather precipitate. May I ask, Miss Richards, why this place holds such an interest for you."

"I have been reading about the Englishwoman Florence Nightingale who went there to nurse sick soldiers, and I wanted to see . . . "

"Laudable and romantic! But don't you think," the cold mocking voice continued, "that you might be better advised to bring your thoughts back from Scutari to this classroom?"

All year long, Linda had done poorly in her work, even though she tried to force herself to study. Latin declensions and German translations did not interest her. Digging her elbows into the table and pressing her hands to her temples, she tried to memorize, but her thoughts wandered far away.

In the Latin class, she felt especially miserable, for the teacher sensed her disinterest and constantly baited her. Now, humiliated by having been made the butt of the teacher's sarcasm, Linda left the room quickly and went to the study hall, which at this moment between classes was empty.

She sat down at one of the tables near the door. As she did so, two girls from the Latin class went by, their voices echoing in the hall.

"Old hawk-eyes certainly roasted that Richards girl," one said.

"Imagine," the other one laughed, "asking that girl to decline the verb *to love*. Do you think she could possibly ever have a beau?"

The Academy was located in a decaying mansion which lay not far from the village green. Here the girls went walking by twos in the afternoons, their full skirts swaying, their bonnets nodding. When they came back, they always talked with excitement of the young men they had glimpsed.

Linda lived with three other girls in a room on

the top floor. The girl that occupied the bed next to her was the daughter of a prosperous draper.

Her name was Pearline. She was pretty, blonde, with a tinkling voice, and she had many beautiful dresses. Bright, able to captivate the teachers, reciting glibly although she seemed never to study, she spent a good deal of time changing the nosegays on her bonnets.

She had an exquisite little workbasket lined with tufted pink silk, many spools of silk thread, a gilt thimble and a beautiful little scissors which she allowed no one to touch.

Although her bed stood only a few feet from Linda's, she scarcely ever spoke to her, nor did the other two girls in the room. At night, all three whispered together about gowns, bonnets, beaux, and treats and assemblies, and Linda who lay staring into the dark felt very lonely.

One night, toward the end of the term, Linda awoke, startled to hear the sound of someone moaning.

She hastily lit her candle and saw that Pearline was sitting up in bed, holding her hand and swaying with pain.

"What is it, Pearline?" she asked. "What has happened to you?"

"I pricked my thumb with the point of my scissors the other day, when I was taking off a ribbon from my bonnet," she answered with a moan and swayed once more with pain.

"The thumb didn't hurt me then at all. But

afterward it began to throb, and it started to feel hot. And now the pain shoots all the way to my shoulder."

Linda put her candle on Pearline's table, and not touching the thumb, for the girl seemed to shrink when she came near her, she saw with concern that it was red, hard and swollen. And from the thumb two angry streaks ran along the arm.

"Oh, dear, oh, dear," moaned the sick girl, "what is going to happen to me?"

"Hush," Linda soothed her. "Nothing is going to happen to you at all."

She knelt by her trunk, rummaged and found what she sought, a sack of flaxseed which she had packed when she left home. She also pulled out a linen hand towel and tore it into several pieces.

"May I use your workbasket?" she whispered.

"Anything, anything, but only do something for this pain which I cannot bear!"

Quickly Linda basted together several little bags, each about as large as the palm of her hand. She filled them loosely with flaxseed and carefully sewed up the edges.

"Now just you lie here and try not to wake the others," she said to the moaning girl who had watched her with anxious interest. "I'll be back in no time at all."

She ran downstairs and a few minutes later came back with a steaming teakettle and a kitchen bowl. She poured boiling water into the bowl and soaked the bags of flaxseed.

Then she took the pillows from her bed, mounded them to make a support for Pearline's aching arm, placing at the top of the pillows several thick, folded towels.

"These will keep the pillows from getting wet."

She wrung out two of the flaxseed poultices, placing them on the pillow side by side so they made a little trough, and asked Pearline to ease her thumb into place between the steaming poultices.

She did so fearfully, screwing up her face with pain, but then she lay back with a sigh. "The heat feels good."

All night long, Linda sat by the girl's bedside, taking away one poultice at a time as it cooled, putting back another that was so hot it stung her fingers as she wrung it out.

From time to time, Pearline dozed. Toward morning she awoke and found Linda beside her. She had brought up another steaming teakettle.

"Are you still there?" she whispered surprised.

"Hush," Linda soothed, and began once more to wring out hot poultices.

When daylight finally came, Linda saw that the red streaks along the girl's arm were fading. And at the side of the thumb, the infection showed white.

Later that day, when Pearline was given permission to see the doctor she insisted on having Linda along. The doctor lanced the thumb and the green suppurative material poured out.

"It's a fine thing," said the bearded physician, "that someone thought to poultice that hand in time. People have died of such infections."

Everyone at school heard what Linda had done, and Pearline became her champion. After that, if anyone had a cut or a scrape they came at once to Linda.

"Will you put on a bit of lint for me? I cut my finger with my penknife and it won't stop bleeding."

"Do you have anything for a toothache? Will oil of cloves really help?"

"I twisted my ankle when I was out in the yard playing darts. Will you put on some hot compresses for me?"

Linda soothed, calmed and comforted anyone at school who got hurt or felt sick. With those who needed her she had always felt at ease.

"How is it," asked Pearline, "that you always know what to do?"

"I really know so very little," Linda sighed. "If I only had some way to learn more."

Somehow the school year came to an end. Although Linda had feared she might not pass, she finally squeezed through the examinations. She went home to visit her grandfather, before going out to seek a post as a teacher.

Chapter V

Linda looked around at the cracked walls of the schoolroom, and then at the gray, November rain which darkened the windows.

"Children, today we will start with sums."

For two years she had been teaching in the school she had attended as a child. Her grandfather had passed away. The farm had been sold for taxes. She "boarded round," receiving part of her pay as "keep."

She taught in one room, with twenty children attending all eight grades. She began each day drearily with an effort, feeling all the time there was some other work she was meant to do.

"Mary Jane," she said, wrapping on her desk with her ferrule, "will you tell me quickly, how much is two times two?"

The little girl did not answer. Her face seemed flushed as if with fever. Instead she said, "My throat hurts," and she began to cry.

"What's the matter, child? Don't you feel well?" Linda put away her ferrule, and bending over the

child who softly whimpered, she felt her forehead.

She rose. "Children, do your sums. Come here to
the window with me, Mary Jane, and let me look
at your throat."

"I feel sick," the little girl complained.

"Open your mouth just a little bit wider." Linda
peered and saw what she had feared—the little
girl's palate and throat were covered with grayish
patches.

It had been a dry summer, followed by a still
drier autumn, the kind of weather apt to bring an
epidemic of diphtheria. In the neighboring village
of Brownington there had already been several
cases, and one child had died.

"We shall have to get you home," she said to the
child.

The little girl drooped against Linda. "I'm too
tired to go home."

Linda spread out her shawl on a bench which
she moved away from the other children, all now
intently interested and craning their necks.

"Children, pay attention to your work!"

She put the little girl on the bench and covered
her carefully with the end of the shawl, wadding
up part of it for a pillow.

Then she sent one of the older boys to fetch
Mary Jane's father, who owned the village feed
store. He was disgruntled when he came into the
schoolroom.

"I can't leave the store," he complained. "What

do you want me here for? A man has to look to his bread and butter first." He scarcely looked at the child.

"Take Mary Jane home and call the doctor."

"The doctor?" His lean, unshaven face wrinkled with horror. "People must think that I'm made of money. That child's always snivelin'. It's probably not much more than a cold."

"I don't like the way her throat looks," Linda explained.

"Teachin' is all that you was hired for!" he snapped back. Lifting the little girl to his shoulder, where her head lay helplessly bobbing, he left the schoolhouse.

Linda went back to her desk. With a sigh she began teaching fractions to the older children, while directing the younger ones to do sums on their slates.

She taught all eight grades in one room. There were two or three children in each grade, and she had to listen to each group in turn, at the same time maintaining discipline, a task which took the concentration of all her powers.

But today she could not keep her mind on her work. She kept thinking of the little girl whom she had scolded that morning, and she wondered if Mary Jane's father would call the doctor.

She dismissed school early and went to inquire after the sick child, who lived with her parents in a weather-beaten cottage at the edge of the village. A timid-looking woman came to the door.

"Mary Jane is feeling very poorly. I've put her to bed."

Although it was November and the weather was chilly, except for a feeble fire in the kitchen stove, the house seemed unheated.

"My husband is saving coal," the woman explained apologetically, holding the apron before her mouth when she spoke to shield the place where her teeth were missing.

She led the way up a narrow stairway to the loft. In a dark room under the eaves, the little girl lay tossing with fever.

"I cover her up," the woman said, "but she keeps throwin' off the covers."

"It's too cold up here for a sick child," Linda indignantly exclaimed. "Light a fire in the parlor and we'll put her down there."

"A fire in the parlor?" Aghast, the startled woman held the edge of her apron against her mouth. "Why, we ain't opened up the parlor since my husband's father died. And then we didn't light a fire. It wasn't needed. Folks just went into the parlor to pay their respects, and then they went out to set in the kitchen."

But with threats and warnings, Linda finally prevailed upon the frightened woman, who opened up the parlor and stood quaking as Linda lit a fire in the tall parlor stove which drew excellently, so that very soon the room became warm.

"I just don't know what my husband will say,"

the woman said shaking her head with a look of deep worry.

"Never mind what your husband will say," Linda directed tersely. "Make up a bed on that horsehair sofa, and I will bring Mary Jane down here."

When the sick child had been settled in the warm room, where she lay with eyes closed, breathing with difficulty, Linda asked, "Have you sent for the doctor?"

"Well, not yet. My husband thought we should wait a bit. You know how the doctor charges. And my husband says the feed business is not so good this year."

Linda snatched up her shawl.

"Where you going, Miss Richards?"

"For the doctor!"

"My husband said we should wait a day or two, that we shouldn't go spendin' before we had to. These fevers can burn themselves out, he says. . . ."

But the door had already slammed. And twenty minutes later, Linda returned with the young physician who had moved into town after old Dr. Currier passed away.

The young man, bustling of manner, bent his dark head, took one look at the child's throat and exclaimed, no doubt in his voice, "It's diphtheria."

Linda sat with the little girl. Toward dark, the child became delirious, and began crying, "I want to go to school to see the teacher."

"Hush," Linda said, "your teacher is here." She

41

put compresses to the child's throat. She tried to get her to take a sip of warm water or weak tea.

The membrane in the child's throat would grow, Linda knew, and if it grew over the windpipe, the child would not be able to breathe. She would choke to death!

Only one thing could save her. Only the child's body, if it was strong enough, could fight the growth of the stifling membrane. Then the membrane, cracking into pieces, could be cast out of the child's throat.

"Please, teacher, don't go!" the sick child whispered in a choking voice. The swelling in her throat made it almost impossible for her to be understood.

Linda remembered with relief that the next day would be Saturday. She took Mary Jane's hot hand. "Don't worry child. I am staying right here with you!"

Mary Jane's father came home and grumbled about the cost of the doctor and the expense of the fire in the stove.

"I don't see why we should be burning up our savings."

Linda left the parlor, closing the door behind her, and faced him infuriated. "It may be cheaper to burn up some wood than to buy a coffin!"

When he had retreated to the bedroom, and his loud snores announced through all the house that he had fallen asleep, his wife, evidently terrorized by her husband, gave Linda some cold baked beans and tepid tea, which she swallowed hurriedly in the kitchen.

Worried about the child, the mother confided to Linda as she gulped the tea, "I lost a child onc't from diphtheria. I watched him chokin' to death."

"Not all children die," Linda assured her.

"I'm glad that you're stayin', even if my husband says that it costs extra to feed you."

Linda went back wearily to the sick child. She did not leave the parlor all night, and she came out in the morning only after the father had gone.

"How is Mary Jane?" the mother asked anxiously, the moment the door had slammed.

"Not worse," Linda told her, "which is all that we can hope for now."

Saturday passed, then Sunday. Linda did not go back to the school on Monday. Several other cases of diphtheria had developed in the town, and the school board in a panic ordered the school closed until the epidemic was over. The epidemic raged. Many children died. Mary Jane was one of the children who survived.

"You saved the child for us," the mother said gratefully.

"We'll never get over the expense," the father complained.

Linda reopened the school and went back to her teaching. She taught decimals and fractions and the multiplication tables. She thought of the children that had died, and she wished that she could have fought with all of her strength for each one of them. The year droned on.

Chapter VI

That summer Linda stayed with Mrs. Poole, an elderly, amiable widow, who lived alone in a neat, white farmhouse, not far from the village.

One day Linda watched the friendly old woman spread out on the table the first square of a patch-work quilt that she was making.

The square, shaped of white fragments, had a red border. In the middle of the square there appeared what seemed to be a child's Christmas tree of blue calico.

"The white stands for purity," the old woman said, "the red stands for love. And this blue tree in the center, that's the tree of life growing."

With a twinkle in her eye, she offered to give the quilt with the tree-of-life pattern to Linda as a wedding present.

"In that case," Linda smiled ruefully, "I am afraid that your quilt will remain a long time quite safely in your possession."

"At nineteen," Mrs. Poole reproved her, "you need hardly regard yourself as a spinster for life."

Shrugging, Linda left the dining room, where the old woman continued to sew thoughtfully on her quilt. Mrs. Poole had no children, only George, a nephew, about whom she spoke frequently.

Several times during the summer he came to visit. He was an eager, vibrant young man, with golden curly hair, and he teased and told jokes constantly.

He ate huge portions of the pies with mountainous meringues which she baked especially for him. She made cookies which he snatched the minute they came out of the oven.

He burst through doors; he swarmed upstairs; he scattered things around. He made the whole house vibrate with excitement. When he left it became abnormally quiet.

Linda was surprised to learn that he made a living by carving gravestones. Once when he left she found scratched on the back of an envelope a sketch for two little stone angels who looked as though they had fallen out of heaven. She couldn't understand him or his outrageous jokes. One day he said, "I make my living only because others oblige me by dying!" Then when a moth tried to fly into the lamp one night, he carried it outside, saying tenderly, "Poor thing, keep on flying."

He talked about all of his girls in Barre. Then one Sunday, he surprised Linda by asking her to go for a ride with him on the *Mountain Maid,* a pleasure boat on Lake Memphremagog.

46

On the boat he was quiet as he sat with Linda at the rail, looking out on the endless blue vista which seemed to blend into the sky.

He told her about his childhood. His parents had died when he was quite young. He had been brought up by his aunt. When he was old enough he was apprenticed to a stonecutter.

Linda wondered why he had chosen such a strange trade, and was about to ask him, when he said, as if reading her mind, "Maybe it's because I'm a lonely person."

"You lonely? How can that be—with all the girls you know?"

"But a man can still be lonely if he's not with the right girl." Then his expression changed and he began to joke, as if to hide what he had said. He puzzled her.

He shimmered, he dazzled. His bubbling and then strangely wistful moods exhausted her. She wished the summer would pass, so she could return to the village where she received part of her salary as a schoolteacher by "boarding round."

Yet when autumn came and Mrs. Poole asked her to stay on, saying, "Your company is worth more than the board to me," Linda found to her own surprise that she wanted to stay. But she insisted on paying for her board.

All winter long, George came and went. "Why, I never knew him to visit so often before," Mrs. Poole remarked with a glance at Linda, who felt her cheeks grow hot. She turned away hastily.

They went sliding on the hills, their sled flying like a bird. They went skating at the edge of the frozen lake, the wind burning their cheeks and numbing their fingers. The air felt like champagne in their lungs, and their hearts beat with excitement.

"The teacher has a beau!" the children whispered in the classroom.

Without knowing how it happened, George and Linda found themselves, at Christmas time, talking of their coming marriage.

"When?" asked Mrs. Poole happily.

"In May," Linda told her, "when school closes."

The busy weeks now sped by with the house in a tumult of sewing and planning. There were towels to hem and pillow cases to make.

Mrs. Poole had almost finished the patchwork quilt. Then she was going to embroider the scallops for the many ruffles on Linda's white wedding dress.

George groaned. "Is this to be a wedding, or a sewing bee?"

March came, then April. A forsythia bush in the corner of the schoolyard burst into sudden, golden bloom, the branches of vibrant color blazing in the sun.

At recess time, some of the little boys brandishing sticks, ran around the bush whacking at each other, scattering the blossoms to the ground.

Linda came out into the yard. "What are you boys doing? You are going to ruin that bush!"

A breathless child, who had fallen into the dirt, picked himself up. "That's not a bush," he cried, "that's Fort Sumter. The Southerners are over there crawling on their bellies. And we're going to show 'em who wants war!"

She shivered. "Come inside and stop your nonsense—all of you!"

A few days later, on the twelfth of April, as she was going home from school, Linda saw a group of men gathered before the printing shop where the village newspaper was issued once a week.

In the window hung a rudely penciled placard: FORT SUMTER HAS BEEN FIRED UPON!

"You'll see," one man cried, "now that Lincoln's in the White House, those erring states won't go in peace!"

"You don't think the president would make war!" another one said. Linda turned away.

Three days later, on the fifteenth of April, another placard hung in the newspaper window, proclaiming that the president had asked for seventy-five thousand militia men from the loyal northern states.

VERMONT WILL BE THE FIRST TO GIVE! the placard read. NO ONE SHALL MARCH BEFORE THE GREEN MOUNTAIN BOYS! The men before the window said jubilantly, "That war can last only a few weeks." The women at the edge of the crowd looked frightened.

George came home from Barre to drill with the militia. Linda put away her wedding dress and sewed on George's uniform. It was a beautiful uniform, with a gray double-breasted coat, cut high in the front and with swooping tails in the back. From shoulder to waist ran two rows of shining brass buttons. On the shoulders glistened epaulets with golden fringe. A gilt star, from which there was suspended a red tassel, was pinned to the breast, and on this star was the inscription, THE VERMONT LIGHT GUARDS.

Every day the men drilled on the village green, marching back and forth with heads held high and arms swinging. From the steps of the little church where she was to have been married, Linda watched them in the afternoons.

"Those uniforms will surely make a fine target for bullets," an old man said, sitting on the steps beside her, squinting as the men marched smartly by.

Linda recognized him. He had fought in the War of 1812. "We didn't bother with uniforms then," he said in a quavering voice, "we just ducked behind the trees and we was glad not to be seen too plain when those bullets came flying." Linda shivered.

The Light Guards who at first had drilled twice a day, now marched and presented arms all day long. The grass in the village green wore down, and in the summer heat that came early that year, clouds of dust rose.

Some people jokingly said the militia would never be called, that the young men drilling would simply wear out their uniforms.

But the day of departure finally came. The Silver Cornet Band struck up a march. The men with sprigs of evergreen in their buttonholes mounted the wagons filled with straw which would take them to Boston.

"Give those rebels a thrashing!" someone cried. "Show Lincoln the Green Mountain Boys are coming!" The cornets blew more loudly. The wagons moved off in the dust.

Linda stayed with Mrs. Poole that summer. The two women did the housework together, ate their meals in silence and waited for letters.

At first the letters were merry. They told of happy ovations in every town through which the militia men passed.

"The women spread tables on the green, and they vie with one another to tempt us with their cooking. I shall never eat bread and butter again. We are offered sometimes as much as ten different kinds of pie."

Then the letters grew a little more serious. "We traveled to Fort Monroe in a tin-pot steamer. The Vermont Light Guards had their first attack of seasickness. Their uniforms are not so beautiful now."

For some time it seemed that the Vermonters would never reach action. Then came a letter from

George telling of the first engagement of the Green Mountain Boys.

"We took part in the action at Big Bethel. We had our first casualty, a boy running through the underbrush beside me. He was hit in the lungs by a sniper. I saw him fall but I had to keep on running. We couldn't stop."

The next letter came a few weeks later. "We don't wear our gay red, gold and gray uniforms. Mine is in tatters and just as well. Plain blue coats and trousers have been issued to us. They don't make quite such a bright target. And we wear a cap with a long visor, to keep the sun from our eyes when we're aiming."

The war which was to have lasted only a few weeks, dragged on. The men from Vermont fought in the Army of the Potomac to protect Washington. They fought at the Battle of Bull Run to turn back the Confederate tide from the capital. They fought again two years later at Gettysburg, where the commander in charge, recognizing Vermont courage, said, "put the Vermonters in front!"

George wrote to Linda, "I have to believe in luck. How else can I explain that I am alive, when so many others have died!"

The loss of men from Vermont was unusually heavy. In the battle at Savage's Station, one Vermont regiment, the Fifth, was wiped out completely. Five brothers, a cousin, a brother-in-law—all from one family—were killed.

When Grant began the Battle of the Wilderness, the First Vermont Brigade, its ranks often thinned, went wearily into the final grim struggle of the war.

Linda received no letters for a long time, and then a letter came from a military hospital near Washington. Linda wept over the note.

George wrote he had been wounded. "It was only a small chest wound. It is all healed now. But it has left me with a cough and with a slight fever which comes on in the afternoons."

On the morning of April 8, 1865, just four years after the firing on Sumter, a message was telegraphed to the village newspaper in Newport. A placard was hung in the window. LEE HAS SURRENDERED!

The church bells rang in the steeples. The women cried, "Have you heard? Have you heard? The men are coming home!"

By twos and threes the men came back, ragged, emaciated, like ghosts. It was late in the summer when George returned. At first, neither Linda nor Mrs. Poole recognized him.

He staggered into the doorway, his eyes sunken, his cheeks hollow, on his face the mark of terrible illness. He swayed forward, "I've come home!"

The women caught him as he fell. They took him upstairs. He lay staring at the yellow light of the candle, at the shadows on the wall. Linda sat beside him, stroking his hand. At length he fell asleep, but from time to time he woke, wrinkling his forehead and moving his lips.

As the days passed he seemed to recover from the daze of his fatigue. He crept downstairs. He sat in a straw chair on the porch, a pillow behind his head, a blanket over his knees. He watched the leaves of autumn falling.

"He'll be better soon, you'll see!" Mrs. Poole told Linda.

Linda noticed that every afternoon the sick man grew feverish. His eyes seemed too big. His face grew thinner, became almost transparent. His cough echoed through the house.

She went on teaching. "Only until you get stronger," she told George, "and then," she put his thin fingers to her lips, "and then we will marry."

During the night she wept, lying on her back, letting the tears run down her cheeks in the dark. It felt good to weep. It untied the knot of misery in her heart. Then she could rise the next day and look calm again.

For five years she nursed the man she loved. She watched him dying of consumption as her mother had died. Finally on a winter night he passed away, crying to Linda, "Help me to live!"

Numbed, she felt only relief that the ordeal was over at last. Weeks passed before the immensity of her loss swept over her, a pain which grew worse each day. When Mrs. Poole passed away suddenly, Linda, looking down at the dead woman, envied her.

Linda left the house where she had once made happy plans for her marriage. She gave to one girl the tree-of-life quilt which Mrs. Poole had made for her. And to another girl, Linda gave the beautiful white dress with scallops which was to have been her wedding dress.

She went on teaching until the end of the school year. She moved like an automaton, sitting in the schoolroom like a ghost.

One day, when the children had gone and the schoolroom was empty, she went to take down her shawl from the peg, and as she did so she caught a glimpse of herself in the wavy mirror that hung on the wall—a woman with a knot of dark hair, her face haggard, around her eyes great circles.

Linda pulled the shawl around her, even though outside an April sun shone, and walking restlessly to her boarding place situated on the other side of town, she found herself stopped by a group of people watching the coach about to leave for Boston.

She saw the driver mounting; she saw the people in the coach waving; and as the wheels began to turn, it came to her bitterly that she had nothing to keep her in Newport but graves.

At the end of the school year she left for Boston, with no plan in mind. As the last glint of Lake Memphremagog disappeared through the trees, Linda began suddenly to speak to an old woman who sat near her. "The hardest thing," she said, "is

55

that I have no one to do for. I have nobody to tend."

The old woman looked at Linda bewildered, as if not understanding what she said, and the coach swept on.

Chapter VII

Several months later, on a dreary day in autumn, Linda stood hesitating before the high, black gate of the Boston City Hospital.

At her boardinghouse, the landlady had told her that women were being hired at this hospital to nurse the city's indigent patients.

Linda buttoned her glove nervously and approached the wicket, where a big, beefy man sat peering out suspiciously. "What do you want?" He barked so rudely that for a moment she could not speak.

She wet her lips. "I have come to seek employment as a nurse."

"The matron hires the ward maids!" He jerked a bloated thumb toward a group of U-shaped buildings which lay in the huge bare yard, surrounded by a high iron fence.

Linda crossed the courtyard, her skirts kicking up the dust. She passed through one door and another; through one building and another and then into the basement of the medical pavilion, along a long green corridor, where the dead air smelled of sickness and dampness.

In a large room lined with shelves and divided by a counter, she found the matron, a stout, flushed woman in a high mobcap, breathing heavily as she threw torn sheets into a cloth spread out on the floor.

She paid no attention to Linda who stood waiting at the counter. Finally, a thin, frightened-looking girl came in. The matron directed her to tie up the bundle of sheets on the floor.

"Take these off to the womens' wards," she ordered, "to be made into shrouds."

Finally she turned to Linda, saying impatiently, "Tell me quickly, what do you want?"

"I have had a good deal of experience in nursing sick people," Linda began somewhat timidly.

The matron swept her with a scrutinizing glance. "Do you drink?" she asked sharply.

Linda gripped the counter. "Of course not!"

The woman made a weary gesture with her hand. "That's what they all say, and then I find them sneaking bottles of grog into the wards. Well I'll tell you one thing, we won't have any drinking in the hospital. The doctors won't stand for it. And the moment that I find out, out you go!"

Linda gasped.

"Where were you in service last?"

"I . . . !"

"Where have you worked—as a housemaid, as a lady's maid? We'll have to have references. We want no one here that's been in trouble with the police."

Linda shook her head. "I have never been in service," she admitted in a low voice.

For the first time in the dim light, the matron noticed Linda's neat black dress and quiet bonnet and looked at her puzzled. "Then what have you done?"

"For the past ten years I have worked as a schoolteacher."

"A schoolteacher!" the matron repeated amazed. "Then what do you want here? We hire housemaids and charwomen. We need women with strong backs that can scrub and lift. This is no work for you."

"I have a strong back!" Linda stubbornly insisted.

The matron was short of help and needed someone right away to work in one of the men's surgical wards. With a shrug of her shoulders she hired the one-time schoolteacher.

Linda had read some years ago of the founding of the Nightingale Training School for Nurses at St. Thomas' Hospital in London. She knew that young women of education in England were being taught by the surgeons and doctors of the hospital to become skilled trained nurses.

But nowhere in America was such training available. However, she was determined that no matter with whom she had to work, or under what conditions, she was going to gain experience as a nurse.

She found herself in a little room between two wards, billeted with three other nurses. The room was so tiny that the two double beds had to be pushed together to make one huge bed, and on this all four women slept.

In the stifling room, the windows were kept shut, and Linda lay tense at the edge of the bed, as far away from the others as she could get.

She never forgot her experience on her first night in this room. The girl lying next to her became violently ill during the night. Linda nursed her as best she could, and wondered at the callousness of the others, who turned their backs and remained undisturbed.

After several repeated nightly experiences, Linda realized the cause of her bedmate's frequent attacks of illness. She discovered a bottle of grog under her pillow.

Linda was assigned to work in a ward for men and boys which had twenty-eight beds. Two girls were put in charge of this ward, each one being responsible for the fourteen beds on her side of the ward.

On her first day of duty, Linda was instructed by the other ward maid, a fat, blowzy girl with stringy hair and puffy eyelids, who also no doubt took recourse each night to the bottle.

"Don't you go running the first time a patient calls you," she warned. "If you do, they'll keep you running all the time, and you'll never get your cleaning done!"

Linda was appalled, but she saw with amazement that as long as the wards were kept spotlessly clean for inspection by the matron, no one seemed particularly concerned about the condition of the patients. They had to fare as best they could with the little care that they received.

Some of the sick brought into the hospital were of the city's homeless. They had no relatives, no one who cared what happened to them.

Sometimes accident cases were brought in from foreign ships docked in the harbor. The hospital grounds stretched to the docks of South Bay, where shipping vessels passed.

One day a Portuguese ship's cook was brought to the hospital. He had broken his back. He lay silent all day long, looking up at the ceiling. He could speak no English.

Linda stopped at his bed whenever she could. As she went flying through the ward, she often felt his tragic eyes turned in her direction.

One day as she passed, he beckoned to her. He had grown very thin, and his eyes looked out from his sunken face as if from the grave.

He pointed feebly to the tall window behind his bed. Linda stood for a moment puzzled. And then she understood. She nodded her head and stroked his hand.

"In just a minute!" she promised.

She went over to the other side of the ward, to

the nurse who was busily dusting the window sills. Linda took out a dollar from her pocket. She had just been paid her wages for the month, seven dollars.

"Will you help me?" she asked.

"For a dollar, of course. What do you want?"

"Help me to turn that man's bed around, so that he can face the window for a little while."

"Whatever for?"

"He wants to look for the last time at the sun."

"Well, you are a queer one!"

They turned the bed around. For an hour the sick man lay looking through the window at the blue sky, in which a few white fleecy clouds drifted by slowly. A smile touched his lips. Some days later he died contented.

Linda carried around in her pocket a thin little book she had bought in a bookstore near Boston Common. It was a book not often seen in America. It was called *Notes on Nursing: What It Is and What It Is Not.* It had been written by Florence Nightingale, when she returned from the Crimea.

It told of the need of the sick for fresh air and dainty food, for company that is not depressing, and especially it told of the deadly effect of drab and monotonous surroundings.

Florence Nightingale was writing of her own experiences when she lay ill with fever in a hut where she had nothing to look at but the knots in the wall. And then she told how the sight of a nosegay of flowers, brought by a soldier who understood the needs of the sick, had turned her from dying to living.

Linda's heart ached for the sick people in her ward, to whom she could not give even the most rudimentary attention, let alone the tender care needed of which Miss Nightingale wrote.

She rose with the other nurses at five in the morning. By five-thirty she was already flying down the long ward, straightening up beds, bringing a cloth with warm water to wash the faces of those who had lain all night long staring into the dark, longing for daylight to come.

She scarcely had a moment to stop at each bedside. Breakfasts coming up on wooden trays from the basement had to be served. Then all the dishes and all the trays had to be washed before they were sent down again.

Twice a day the long ward and the halls had to be swept. If the charwomen did not come, then the two nurses together washed down the ward.

Every day all the beds and the window sills had to be wet dusted, wiped off with a soapy rag and then polished with a dry cloth so that streaks would not show.

At ten o'clock when the doctors came to change dressings, Linda followed the dresser with a pail into which he threw all the soiled bandages which he took off of the wounds.

Of course the wound became infected, and

drained for many long weeks before it could heal. Sometimes the infection continued so long that the patient was worn out and died of exhaustion. Or if the infection spread into the bloodstream, then death came from blood poisoning.

A Scottish surgeon, Joseph Lister, believed that Pasteur's invisible germs caused these infections. The doctors in America did not credit this belief, contending that if the patient were strong enough, his wounds would heal, otherwise not.

After the rounds with the dresser, Linda took all the soiled bandages to a sink off one of the wards, washing by hand those which could be made white again. Then she hung the bandages up in the attic to dry, looping them over long dusty clotheslines strung up for this purpose.

Every afternoon, for hours at a time, she stood at a padded table in the hallway off the ward, ironing the yards and yards of bandages which had to be rolled up again for use the next day.

When a patient called her from the other end of the ward, she hastily put back her iron on the little gas heating grill which she had near her table, and ran the full length of the ward to tend him.

The other nurse complained. "You are spoiling the patients. Why don't you let them know that you can't come running every minute?"

One boy particularly concerned Linda. A chimney sweep, he had hurt his leg in a fall while at work, and the long abrasion had drained for weeks. He had grown so thin that one day when he showed his arm to a woman visiting in the ward, she fainted.

The doctors had nicknamed him Spindly. Although he was fourteen years old, and tall for his age, Linda had heard one of the doctors say that Spindly weighed only forty pounds.

The odor from his wound was dreadful and the boy, white to the lips, refused his food when Linda brought him the hospital tray. But she coaxed him with fresh fruit that she bought from the green grocer on Harrison Avenue, with toast that she made for him on the gas ring, and with jelly she had brought with her from Vermont.

At night, when the lights were turned out in the ward, she sat at his bedside. She told him how the children used to go skating on frozen Lake Memphremagog, how in summer a steamer took passengers across the lake.

"Is it big like an ocean?" he asked, putting out his hand so she could hold his thin fingers.

"Not as big as an ocean," she told him in a whisper, "but still very large. On all sides the lake is surrounded by mountains."

"I should like to see the mountains," he declared in a wistful whisper, "before I die."

When he became very weak and could not call her from the other end of the ward, she brought him a little silver bell; and no matter how often he rang it, she came running.

Sometimes he rang, even if he did not need her,

saying with a wan smile when she came, "I just wanted to know you were there!"

She never scolded him when he did this, no matter how much she had to do, but tweaked his ear gently and called him by pet names, or if he begged she told him a story.

"Tell me the story of the frog!"

Over and over again she had to tell him the story of the frog with the broken leg, and how she had made a little splint for his leg and had fed him flies until he got well.

"Why don't you make me well?" he sometimes said sadly.

"But the frog gobbled up every fly that I brought him, and you, you naughty boy, didn't even look at your supper!"

At night, when it was time to put out the lights in the ward, Spindly always became very sad. "Don't leave me," he begged. "I am afraid I will die."

"But Spindly, you know that it is forbidden for the nurses to stay in the wards. If I'm found here in the night, I will be discharged. And then who will take care of you?"

At night a night watcher came. The night watcher was usually a charwoman who worked all day somewhere, and then went out at night to watch in the hospital in order to earn a few extra pennies. Often she spent these pennies on a bottle of grog which she brought into the hospital; and, then, intoxicated, she slept with her head on her arms, not hearing the patients, who sometimes died without help.

Linda worried about Spindly, and each night she asked the night watcher to listen for his bell. The night watcher promised. Then one night, though the other patients said the sick boy rang, the night watcher, deep in a drunken sleep, did not hear him, and Spindly died as he had feared he might, with no one near him.

Linda wept, and each time when she passed the bed from which he used to call, she felt heartbroken all over again. She could not eat or sleep. She grew thin. One morning she woke with a raging fever. She had contracted typhus.

For weeks she lay ill in one of the women's wards, delirious, not knowing where she was. When the fever left her, the nurse who had cared for her, a stout Irish woman, spoke to her curiously.

"Who was that Spindly you were calling for?" she asked.

Linda told the nurse of the boy who had died.

"I know how you feel," said the Irishwoman. Her name was Rosa McCormick. She had been working in the hospital since it was founded. "That was in 1864, the year the war ended," she said. "It's almost eight years now."

She crossed her plump arms over her ample bosom. "I've seen a lot of sufferin' and a lot of dyin'. We do what we can. There's no use grievin' for what can't be helped."

Linda looked at the nurse, a kind, decent woman. There was a great deal that Linda wanted to say, but she felt too weak to gather her thoughts, and fearing she might cry if she spoke of Spindly again, she wearily closed her eyes.

When Linda recovered from her illness, she left the hospital. She went to live with a distant relative in Foxboro, and there, weary, drained of emotion, she worked for a time in a hat factory.

This dreary existence at last appalled her, and on Saturday afternoons she began to take the steam cars to Boston, where she rummaged in the dim little bookshops near Boston Common. She always stopped to read if she found a book on nursing, and more and more frequently she bought these books and took them home.

Chapter VIII

On a hot Saturday afternoon, in the summer of 1872, as Linda aimlessly browsed in a Boston bookshop, she stopped at the bulletin board near the door.

There among the announcements of rooms to rent, and of lectures on phrenology to which the public was invited, she saw posted a small, cheaply printed light green handbill.

She read the handbill twice, then took the omnibus to Pleasant Street, where she got off before a row of red brick dwellings connected by wooden passages.

Before one of these houses hung a sign, printed in gold, announcing: THE NEW ENGLAND HOSPITAL FOR WOMEN AND CHILDREN: WOMEN PHYSICIANS IN ATTENDANCE

Linda went inside and asked for the resident physician. A neat maid ushered her into a pleasantly furnished parlor. A few minutes later the sliding doors opened to admit the most beautiful young woman Linda had ever seen.

"I am Dr. Susan Dimock," she said.

She was dressed in a plain dark gown fastened high at the throat with a cameo pin. Her brown hair, parted in the center, was drawn back smoothly into a heavy bun at the back of her neck. A faint pink color glowed in her cheeks.

She sat down at a small mahogany desk near the window. Leaning forward on her arms, a friendly smile on her face, she said to Linda, "What can I do for you, Miss Richards?"

Linda rose. "Is it true," she asked nervously wetting her lips, "that you intend to open at this hospital a one-year course to train nurses?"

"Ah," cried the young woman doctor, "then you must have read one of the handbills which I posted only this morning. Yes, it is quite true. We shall open a school to train nurses this autumn, just as soon as we have moved our hospital to the new building which is being erected for us in Roxbury."

"May I enroll now?"

The beautiful young woman gave Linda a radiant smile. She took out from her desk a brand new ledger. "In that case," she said, "you will be our first student!"

Eager to begin, Linda spent the summer working with Dr. Dimock in the hospital. She learned of the valiant struggle which the women physicians had put up to achieve their education and to establish a place where they could practice.

She met the founder of the hospital Dr. Marie

Zakrzewska, a tall, grim Polish woman with gray hair and sharp features. She had given her life to the training of women physicians.

"Just because something has not been done," she said with her explosive Polish accent, "does not mean that it cannot be done!"

She had been the chief midwife in the Berlin charity hospital, but had been unable to gain entry to a medical school. Hearing that an American woman had been graduated as the first woman doctor, Marie Zakrzewska came to New York, where she made her living by sewing.

Finally she found Dr. Elizabeth Blackwell, the first woman doctor, who helped her get to a medical school in Cleveland, which would admit a woman student.

When Dr. Zakrzewska was graduated, she worked with Dr. Blackwell, and together they founded the New York Infirmary for Women and Children, one of the first hospitals to be operated by women physicians.

Then Dr. Zakrzewska came to Boston, where she taught in a little medical school for women. But her graduates could not be admitted to Boston hospitals to practice, so ten years ago she founded a little hospital to which the women doctors could bring their patients.

Of all of her graduates, Dr. Zakrzewska considered the young southern girl Dr. Susan Dimock the most brilliant. This young woman had been studying medicine since she was fifteen years old. She had a natural gift for surgery and was flawless in her work in anatomy and dissection.

Dr. Zakrzewska sent Susan Dimock, at her own expense, to finish her studies in surgery at the University of Zurich in Switzerland, now admitting women to this course.

Completing her work there at the age of twenty-six, Dr. Dimock had stopped off to visit at Kaiserwerth. There she studied the methods of the famous Fliedners, a Lutheran minister and his wife who had started the first hospital to train deaconess nurses. Florence Nightingale had come to this hospital for her inspiration.

Then in London, Dr. Dimock stopped to visit with Mrs. E. S. Wardroper, the famous matron of St. Thomas' Hospital, chosen by Florence Nightingale to direct the Nightingale Training School for Nurses.

When Dr. Dimock came back to America to undertake her work as resident physician and surgeon of the New England Hospital for Women and Children, she told Dr. Zakrzewska, her chief, that she wanted to found a training school for nurses, using the same methods employed by Florence Nightingale.

Dr. Dimock told Linda one evening that previous efforts had been made to train nurses in America. "Others tried before, but it may be that the time was not yet ripe. An idea has to grow."

In 1798, a New York surgeon, Dr. Valentine Seaman, had called his nurse attendants together in the New York Hospital, to teach them how to take care of obstetrical patients.

Dr. Joseph Warrington, a Quaker physician, had tried in his Philadelphia home to train women to go out to do home nursing. Mainly he tried to teach midwifery and the care of infants.

Then in 1863 a women's hospital in Philadelphia took out a charter for a school to train nurses. But in ten years they obtained only one student, and she stayed only six months. No diploma had been granted.

"I shall remain," Linda promised, "until I receive mine!"

She helped Dr. Dimock and Dr. Zakrzewska remove the patients to the new hospital building set high on a hill in Roxbury, a suburb of Boston. There, four more students enrolled in the school of nursing: Caroline Stapfer, Molesca Woods, Miss Thayer and Mrs. Wolhaupter, a young widow.

The course of training was to be one year. The nurses were to receive an allowance of one dollar a week. No uniform was required. "A calico housedress and felt slippers will do," Dr. Dimock told the young women.

The new hospital structure, a three-story building of dark red stone, with pointed green towers and a gloomy port-cochere, looked rather like a medieval castle. Inside, however, the hallways were wide, and the rooms which had high ceilings and long windows were filled with sunshine.

The hospital had room for seventy-five patients,

two in a room. Between every two rooms, a nurse slept in a thin slice of a bedroom, the doors at either side standing open at night, so the patients whom she had tended all day could call her during the night.

Linda was given such a room on the second floor. She cared for her patients all day; she was on call all night. Sometimes she rose as many as a dozen times a night. Sometimes she did not lie down at all, and became so exhausted that on one occasion she did a fantastic thing.

She had been taking care of a woman who was gravely ill and when the woman finally passed away in the middle of the night, it was Linda's duty to take the body to the basement, where a small room beyond the coal bin served as a morgue.

In the creaking lift, Linda swayed with weariness, and the candle in her hand almost went out. Finally she deposited her burden on the table in the morgue. In a cold sweat of exhaustion she sat down for just a moment and fell asleep with the burning candle in her hand. The hot drippings of the candle on her hand awakened her, and she fled to her room.

Some days later, when Linda told this story to the classmate who worked across the hall, the girl burst into tears.

"I cannot go on in this way," she sobbed, "working in the daytime and then staying up at night!"

"Let me take care of your patients tonight, while

you sleep," Linda suggested. "And tomorrow night you may do the same for me."

This worked out so successfully that Linda went to Dr. Dimock's office to suggest this as a working plan for all the nurses. "Sometimes we become so weary for lack of sleep," she said, "that we hardly know what we are doing."

Dr. Dimock was sympathetic but also adamant. "I will not bring night watchers into this hospital!"

Linda was equally obstinate. "I am merely suggesting that if one nurse slept while the other one took care of her patients, we all could take turns in this way."

Dr. Dimock regarded her thoughtfully. "I will consider the matter." Several days later she called Linda to her office. "We will institute your plan!"

The nurses began to take turns at the nightwork, and then, in January, a new nurse was hired to take charge of all patients at night. In this way the practice of night nursing was instituted.

"You have the ability of organization," Dr. Dimock told Linda, when she saw how successful the plan was.

During the winter, the hospital physicians gave lectures on medical matters to the students in nursing. Dr. Zakrzewska spoke on general nursing. The twins, Emily and Augusta Pope, gave four lectures on physiology. Dr. Lucy Sewall gave a talk on preparing food for the sick. Dr. Emma Call gave instruction on contagious nursing and Dr. Helen Morton on childbed care.

Dr. Dimock, who lectured on surgical nursing, told of the wonders of ether anesthesia discovered in Boston by William Thomas Greene Morton, a dentist. "Once surgery was confined only to the surface of the body. The surgeon could take only a moment or two to perform an amputation or remove an exterior growth, because of the terrible pain.

"But now that the patient can be put to sleep and feels no pain, we are not afraid to probe beneath the surface, inside the body." She went on to say that at the Massachusetts General Hospital, for the first time in medical history, a daring surgeon had removed a diseased appendix. "That date, 1870," she said, "will go down in history!"

She permitted the nurses to watch her performing an autopsy, and she also allowed chosen ones to come into surgery to witness operations. She never seemed to lose her head in emergencies.

Linda was at work with her in the dispensary one day, when a boy of eight brought in his little brother of five who had just chopped off the tip of his finger, almost at the joint.

Dr. Dimock tapped the older boy on the head. "Tell me, noodle-head," she said smiling, "where did you drop the top of that finger?" He stared at her in amazement. "Now run home and get it for me just as fast as you can!"

When he returned with the missing part, she

fitted it on neatly, carefully set the fracture, then tied the two parts of the finger together in a splint. Before long the patched-up finger healed so perfectly that very little scar showed. If it had not healed, she said, the result would have been gangrene. "But a surgeon has to take a risk sometimes!"

She told the nurses that their very thoughts could influence a patient. "You must never give up. You must never let yourself feel hopeless."

During the winter there was an epidemic of pneumonia. So many patients fell ill with this disease that some of them could not be taken into the hospital. They had to be nursed at home.

Dr. Dimock sent Linda to nurse a woman who seemed to be dying. She lay propped on pillows, her face blue for lack of oxygen, fighting for breath.

Linda tilted the woman forward and put on a huge jacket poultice, applying it steaming hot to her chest and back. Over and over again, Linda put on the hot poultice, an ordeal for the woman's heart, but the only means known for fighting the infection.

For six days and six nights, Linda fought for the woman's life. On the seventh day, as she approached the bed with the steaming poultices which she had just soaked in hot water, the sick woman turned her head on the pillow.

"Leave me alone," she whispered, "I can't struggle any more."

Linda found herself speaking almost with anger. "What do you mean," she demanded, "by giving up? You have a family. Your children need you!" And she continued to apply the hot poultices, determined to go on until either the woman died or revived. An hour passed, an hour of grim, gasping struggle.

Then suddenly the woman's breathing became more normal. The blue, choked look left her face. Her temperature dropped. A light perspiration broke out on her forehead.

When Dr. Dimock came she said with approval, "The crisis has passed. You have done what a nurse can sometimes do even better than the doctor. You have saved this woman's life!"

Linda returned to the hospital, and the busy weeks passed rapidly. She left the hospital grounds only twice all year, once at Christmas time and once at Easter, when she was given permission to go to church in Boston.

Spring came, then summer and then the first golden days of autumn. On the first of September, exactly one year after she had started her training, Dr. Dimock sent for Linda.

It was about ten o'clock in the morning when Linda, who had been giving baths to her patients, went down hurriedly in her calico dress and felt slippers. Around her waist she had tied a flowered gingham apron with a deep pocket which she liked to wear when on duty.

She stood before Dr. Dimock's desk. "Is there something you want of me?"

"No," said the woman physician with a mystifying smile. "I have something which I want to give you, something which I hope you will treasure all your life!" From the drawer in her desk she took out a scroll of stiff white paper, imprinted with black script and embossed with a golden seal.

"What is this?" Linda asked.

"Your diploma!"

The two women shook hands. Linda put the scroll in her pocket and went upstairs to take care of her patients. Later, sitting on the edge of the bed in her room, Linda studied the document which said that on September 1, 1873, Melinda Ann Judson Richards, having completed her training at the New England Hospital Training School, "is now duly qualified to practice her profession as a trained nurse."

The little graduation exercise, held without ceremony, did not go unnoticed. Soon letters came to the New England Hospital for Women and Children, asking for the services of America's first trained nurse.

A group of women trying to start a training school for nurses at the Massachusetts General Hospital needed a director.

The Hartford Hospital desired the services of a trained nurse for their surgical ward. And at Bellevue Hospital in New York, where a Nightingale school to train nurses had just been started, a night superintendent was needed.

Linda decided on the latter post. At the back of her mind perhaps lay the recollection of suffering she had seen in a great city hospital, when the dying lay alone and unattended at night.

Before Linda left, Dr. Zakrzewska offered her the position of head nurse at the New England Hospital for Women and Children.

Linda went to discuss this offer with Dr. Dimock, whom she had grown to love and with whom she longed to stay. "I would like to remain here, and yet I feel that where I am going I may be needed more."

"Then tell them at Bellevue," said Dr. Dimock with a radiant smile, but in a voice that trembled slightly, "tell them we proudly send them our first graduate!"

Linda left for New York.

Chapter IX

The old, soot-covered buildings of Bellevue Hospital rose behind iron gates, in a swampy area near the East River.

To this hospital, once an almshouse and prison, the city's indigent sick were brought—the dazed, the hurt, the insane. Here great abuses once existed.

The nurses were drunken wanderers, picked up from the streets by the police and condemned to work off their sentences at Bellevue. They were called "ten-day women." They drank the medicines of the patients and fought in the wards.

When a group of charitable ladies heard of these horrors, they sent Elizabeth Hobson, one of their members and a woman of refinement, to investigate.

A young Bellevue surgeon Dr. Gill Wylie, on duty in the wards, whispered to Mrs. Hobson, "Go look in the bathroom!"

She opened the door and almost fainted at what

she saw—the bathtub filled with unspeakable rub-
bish, and on a pile of filthy rags, a drunken "nurse!"

She saw dinner served, hunks of dried fish and
bread, brought up in a newspaper, dumped out on
a dirty table and carried to the bedsides of the sick
in the hands of fellow patients!

Sick at what she had seen, Mrs. Hobson reported
to the ladies' committee. They prevailed on the
commissioner to let them start a nursing school at
their own expense, "to improve the nursing service
at the hospital." They were granted the use of six
wards.

The young surgeon Dr. Gill Wylie, who had
spoken to Mrs. Hobson, offered to go to England
to consult Florence Nightingale.

He found Miss Nightingale ill and unable to see
him. But he saw Mrs. Wardroper, the famous
matron of St. Thomas' Hospital. As superintendent
of the Nightingale Training School, she allowed
him to observe the methods approved by Miss
Nightingale.

When Dr. Wylie returned to Bellevue, he found
a letter from Miss Nightingale, a letter of instructions and encouragement, which became a consti-
tution for the first Nightingale school to be set up
in America.

The "lady managers" of the school faced many
difficulties, the principal one being that a suitable
superintendent for the school could not be
found.

In the house on Twenty-Sixth Street, which the

ladies had rented as a home for their nurses, Mrs. Hobson ordered that a bed should be made ready for the superintendent, saying hopefully, "Someone will come!"

A few days after that bed was made up, on a May morning in 1873, a stout woman in black nunlike robes mounted the steps of the nurses home, a silver crucifix hanging at her side.

She was Miss Helen Bowdoin, known in England as Sister Helen. A member of the All Saints Sisterhood, an Anglican order in London, she had come to Baltimore to visit a branch of the sisterhood. And there she had heard of the new training school being founded at Bellevue.

With tears in her eyes, Mrs. Hobson accepted the offer of Sister Helen to become the first superintendent of nurses at Bellevue.

Sister Helen soon brought order into the wards. A calm, inscrutable woman, her waxen face framed by a white linen coif, Sister Helen awed everyone in the hospital, scaring even the politicians who once had battened on the sick.

In a little room off one of the wards, she sat in a big, black leather chair trimmed with tassels, writing orders for nurses and patients.

On a gray October day, Linda stood before her, newly arrived from Boston and eager to take over her duties as night superintendent.

"Spend as many days as you wish in the wards," Sister Helen told her. "Go from bed to bed. When you know all the hundred patients to be put in your charge at night, return to me. Do not come back until you know each and every case."

Linda returned two days later.

"So soon?" asked Sister Helen.

"Yes, Sister, I am ready."

Sister Helen looked at the wall where there hung the framed letter from Miss Nightingale. And then in a cool voice, she gave Linda her instructions.

"You are to see each head nurse before she leaves for the night, and you are to take from her all orders for the care of her patients."

"Yes, Sister."

"You are to give all medicines. You yourself are to take care of those who grow worse or who seem seriously ill. Only you can send for the house physician at night."

"I understand, Sister."

"You are to instruct the nurses in their duties every hour. And in the morning as each head nurse comes on duty, you shall report to her what has transpired during the night."

"It shall be done, Sister."

"One more thing. From time to time you may bring me notes that you make about the most interesting cases for which you have cared, so I may know what is going on in the hospital."

"I shall do so, Sister."

Without turning her face, Sister Helen went on, "If we can prove by the superiority of our nursing that the patients fare better, and the work of the doctors is facilitated, then the work of the training school may someday be extended to the other wards of the hospital."

"I shall do my best, Sister."

Linda began her work in the wards that night. She was to write later, "I shall never forget my first experiences on night duty at Bellevue. The long, ghostly wards, the echoing sound of distant footsteps, the moans of the sick were to remain forever in my memory.

"No sooner had the day nurses left the wards than the gas began to burn so low that the faces of the patients could not be distinguished. One could see only the dim outlines of figures wrapped in gray blankets lying upon the beds. If any work was to be done, a candle had to be lighted, and only two candles a week were allowed in each ward.

"At midnight all the steam was turned off. At three in the morning it was turned on again, and the crackling of the pipes would waken everyone in the wards.

"How cold and how dismal were the hours between midnight and three o'clock in the morning! The captain of the night watch made several rounds of the wards through the night, and at five in the morning he turned off all gas, leaving the hospital in darkness until morning."

The patients with pneumonia, or those recovering from recent operations, could not be uncovered in the cold wards. By candlelight a saturated dressing could not easily be changed. The greatest difficulty was in dealing with accident cases brought in at night.

In spite of all complaints by Linda to Sister Helen, and all complaints by Sister Helen to the warden, the answer always came back, "The commissioners will not permit us to waste gas or heat at night."

The hospital had a horse-drawn ambulance, the first vehicle of its kind in the country introduced by Dr. Edward Dalton, a surgeon who had served in the Civil War, when he came to work at Bellevue. He urged that the injured in the city streets be picked up as promptly as the wounded on the battlefields. He designed a wagon, shielded by black leather curtains, in which splints, bandages and medical supplies for emergencies—as well as a litter—could be stored.

But his notion was opposed by the city commissioners until one night a man was wounded by stabbing and lay on the floor of a saloon for five hours, his intestines gaping. He died before a wagon could be hired at a livery stable to take him to the hospital. Then the ambulance which Dr. Dalton had designed was put into service at Bellevue.

At night Linda could hear the bell clanging, as the horse-drawn vehicle, kept in a barn near the morgue, went racing from the gates of the hospital. Emergency cases were usually brought to her wards, where the great difficulty lay in taking care of these cases by insufficient light.

Linda Richards

One night the stretcher-bearers brought in a man badly burned in a tenement fire. His clothes were singed, his face was black. He looked more like a burnt log than a human being.

Linda bent over the litter, cutting away the hurt man's garments. Great patches of burnt cloth adhered to his skin.

The surgeon, coolly directing that the man should be kept from shock, had gone off to bed. The nurse in the ward held up a half-burnt out candle over Linda as she worked.

"Get ready a bath of soda solution," Linda told her. Together they lowered the injured man into the tub to soak away the cloth that adhered.

As they did so the glimmering candle went out. Somehow in the darkness the two women pulled the man from the tub. Somehow they managed to wrap him in sheets wrung in soda solution and then in blankets.

They carried him to a bed. They surrounded him with bed warmers. They poured hot, sweet liquids down his throat. They waited for morning, not knowing if he lived or died. When the first light of morning came, Linda saw that by some miracle the hurt man still breathed.

She went shaking with anger to see Sister Helen. "I will not work another night under such conditions!" Linda cried.

For a moment, Sister Helen did not speak. Her mouth twitched slightly. Then she told Linda, "You may go to the warden."

87

Linda poured out her wrath on this bland gentleman who, spreading out fat fingers, tried to soothe her.

"Now don't be upset, Miss Richards! Now don't be upset!"

"Upset?" she cried. "It is you who will be upset when I go to the city commissioners, if that man in the ward should die!"

The warden put his hand to his face. "If you will promise that the nurses will not waste gas," he offered, "we might try to leave the gas on for a few nights." There was no lack of light after that at Bellevue!

When Linda made her rounds in the night, she sometimes found a patient, apparently recovering during the day, who showed suddenly an alarming change. Usually this happened with patients worn out by long illness, but no longer thought to be in danger.

She came on such a patient one night, or rather before dawn, during that hour between three and four when the powers of the sick seem to be at the lowest.

He lay propped on the pillows, his face suddenly pinched, his eyes deeply sunken, his pulse at a hundred and thirty, very thready and like no pulse at all, but rather like a string just faintly vibrating under the skin. He breathed in short gasps. His limbs turned icy and he seemed to be dying!

Yet the next morning when the day nurses came on duty, this patient, sitting up in bed, his face no longer pinched, his eyes no longer sunken, seemed so normal that they would not believe Linda when she told them what had happened.

She tried to impress on the day nurse the need to inform the doctor. Florence Nightingale had written of such cases, saying, "The patient who seems to be dying at night, yet recovers in the daytime, must be carefully watched.

"The doctor who does not see the patient at his worst," she warned, "may not know his true condition, unless the nurse can briefly and clearly put the situation of the sick person before him."

"Cases like this," the great nurse predicted, "often go off rather suddenly, from some trifling ailment of a few days, which adds just sufficient exhaustion to cause death."

It happened just this way with Linda's patient, who passed away suddenly because the day nurses, not believing her, had not warned the doctors of his condition. She wondered how she could signal the doctors in such cases.

She came to the hospital each night, an hour before she had to go on duty, and going from ward to ward she gathered information on the state of the patients during the day. She asked so many questions that sometimes the day nurses became cross.

"It would take a penny notebook," one of them cried impatiently, "to answer all the questions you ask!"

The next evening Linda brought penny notebooks and she tied them to the beds of several gravely sick patients. She begged the nurses to put down temperatures and pulse rates.

"Then I won't have to ask you so many questions."

A few complied.

After a time, studying one of these notebooks in which records had been kept for several days, she wished for some way to make a patient's progress visible at a glance. As she stood pondering, a sick seaman lying on the bed watching her, remarked, "What are you trying to do, chart my course?"

That night, when she had a few minutes to sit down at her desk, she quickly ruled off a sheet of paper into little squares. And on this roughly made chart paper, she plotted the temperature and the pulse rate of a patient who had been ill for some time.

Then holding off the chart, she studied the jagged mountain peaks and valleys she had drawn. Now she could see visibly before her the patient's day-by-day progress.

She began to keep charts for several patients. From time to time she was obliged to hand in to Sister Helen a written report on some interesting case. Linda did so, including a chart of the patient's pulse beat, temperature, respiration and other information which could be shown graphically.

Sister Helen looked at the chart puzzled. "What is this?"

Linda explained. "It is a way that I have devised

to make the patient's progress visible at a glance."

"H-mmm," said Sister Helen, and from her expression Linda could not tell what the superintendent of nurses thought.

A few days later, Sister Helen called Linda to her office. On her desk lay the chart. She took it up with puffy fingers.

"The doctors have studied this chart," she said, her face as usual inscrutable. "And it is their wish that such records should be kept for all the patients."

In this way there began at Bellevue a method of chart keeping, later copied by other hospitals, and used to this day, in all parts of the world, to save lives.

That spring an epidemic of childbed fever broke out in the maternity wards. These wards of the hospital had never been turned over to the nursing school. Ignorant, untrained women still served as nurses in these wards, where the mothers died without proper care.

The "lady managers" of the nursing school pleaded with the medical board. "Let us send in properly trained nurses to take care of the dying mothers."

The medical board refused. The "lady managers" organized public meetings. Petitions were signed, prominent citizens lent their aid.

Grudgingly the board agreed, but imposed what many thought might be an impossible condition.

"The school must furnish a trained nurse, experienced in obstetrics, to direct the work."

Sister Helen interviewed Linda in the presence of the "lady managers." She asked Linda if it were true that she had taken her training under the well-known specialist in obstetrics, Dr. Marie Zakrzewska of Boston?

"Quite true," Linda replied.

"And while training at the New England Hospital for Women and Children, where Dr. Zakrzewska was the principal *accoucheuse,* did you receive any experience in maternity nursing?"

"I worked for three months in the maternity cottage to which no other type of cases were admitted," answered Linda.

Sister Helen looked at the "lady managers" who nodded their heads. A few hours later, Linda was relieved of her duties as night superintendent and went to take charge of the maternity wards.

There Linda found an atmosphere of dread. She was appalled to discover that the women waiting to have babies were obliged to sit in their beds and sew shrouds for the dead.

She told the warden, "I will not permit the sight of another shroud in the wards. What do you want to put into these women's heads—the thought of dying? Are they not terrified enough?"

She did everything she could to make the wards clean and cheerful. She was present at the birth of every baby. In twenty-seven days, twenty-seven babies were born, most of them arriving at night.

She watched the mothers. She tried to soothe their fear. But the fever struck in bed after bed. The women died screaming, delirious.

Worn out, shaking with fatigue, one day Linda dared to say to the attending doctor, "We had no such deaths at the New England Hospital for Women and Children."

"Why not?"

"Because the maternity cases were kept in a separate building, and no doctor could go near them who had handled an autopsy or a wound."

"Germs! Bah!" he cried. "We do not credit the fantastic ideas of Dr. Oliver Wendell Holmes. That paper he wrote is nonsense!"

More women died. The papers called Bellevue "a slaughterhouse for mothers." The terrified women refused to come to the hospital to have babies.

The maternity wards finally had to be closed. In a charity hospital on Blackwell Island, temporary wards were opened. The women had to be taken across the East River on a ferryboat.

Linda served on this boat, and also in the rough shed on the dock where many babies were born, because the mothers, fearing the hospital, waited in terror until the last moment.

The mothers who had their babies on the dock refused, no matter how badly they felt, to go on to the hospital. And returned to their homes, they did not die.

"Can't you see," Linda pleaded, "that it is the doctors themselves who carry the infection from other cases in the hospital?"

Many years were to pass before this idea could be accepted. Then when doctors began to take proper precautions, the deadly disease vanished and no more mothers died.

Finally the epidemic of childbed fever at Bellevue burnt itself out. The emergency wards on Blackwell Island were closed, the Bellevue wards reopened.

Linda went back to her duties as night superintendent. That summer Sister Helen went to London to study the Nightingale methods practiced at St. Thomas' Hospital.

When she returned, she gave examinations to all the students in training. Linda and Mrs. Wohlhaupter, a nurse from the New England Hospital who had joined her at Bellevue, also took these examinations.

Happily, Linda wrote to her old teacher Dr. Susan Dimock, "You would be proud of us. We passed the Nightingale examinations without effort!"

At the end of the summer, Sister Helen offered Linda the post of assistant superintendent, which meant that when Sister Helen left, as she was planning to do in a year or two, that Linda would become superintendent.

She refused this flattering offer. A group of women, long struggling to start a school to train nurses at the Massachusetts General Hospital in Boston, had written to her for help.

"But what if that school should fail?" asked Sister Helen.

Linda shook her head, meeting the other one's look with her own level glance. "You did not fail at Bellevue."

Chapter X

As she was passing through the wards a few days after she undertook her duties at the Massachusetts General Hospital, Linda noticed a nurse polishing the brass knobs on one of the beds.

On the bed lay a sick man, his eyes partly closed, his mouth sagging strangely. Linda beckoned to the nurse. "How long has that man been in that condition?"

"In what condition?" asked the nurse, a buxom girl with rosy cheeks, drops of perspiration standing out on her forehead.

"How long have you worked in this hospital?" Linda asked.

"Two years."

"Two years? And you do not know when a patient is dying!"

"Dying?" the girl said amazed. "I had not noticed!"

"Get the doctor immediately," Linda ordered. "Put screens around the bed. And do not leave that poor man so long as he needs you!"

Linda found the hospital wards immaculately clean. On every bed lay a snowy spread, on every table a doily glazed with starch. The women's beds were shielded by dimity curtains which hung in perfect folds.

The Massachusetts General Hospital was not far from the noted eminence of Beacon Hill. Green lawns stretching down to the Charles River surrounded the imposing building with its high dome and stately columns modeled after the State House.

This hospital founded by Dr. John Collins Warren had long been noted for the courage and the fame of its surgeons. Dr. Henry J. Bigelow, a surgeon of distinguished family, had encouraged Morton's experiments with anesthesia. In the ether dome of the hospital, the first operation with ether anesthesia had been performed.

Dr. Warren and Dr. John Homans, experimenting with Lister's carbolic spray to prevent surgical infection, started all their operations by saying, "Gentlemen, let us spray!"

Dr. Reginald Heber-Fitz, daring the adventure of abdominal surgery, had for the first time taken out a perforated appendix, until then always a cause of death.

These men of courage, however, had remained unmoved when Dr. Samuel David Gross of Pennsylvania had called in a medical paper "for the establishment of schools for the education of nurses."

In his "manifesto for nursing" read before a

meeting of the American Medical Association held in 1869 in New Orleans, Dr. Gross warned, "It will be difficult a half a century hence to account for our utter apathy on this subject!"

The surgeons of the Massachusetts General Hospital, an institution gleaming with cleanliness, felt no want in the care of their patients.

A few years later, however, the trustees of the hospital felt moved by delicate considerations to indulge the whim of a lady, who asked the use of three wards for the training of nurses.

The lady was Mrs. Samuel Parkman, the widow of a surgeon who long had been an honored member of the staff of the Massachusetts General Hospital.

He had died of typhoid fever at his home, during an epidemic when another member of his family also lay ill. His wife had not been able to secure nurses, except for some clumsy medical students sent to her by the medical college. Greatly moved by the need she had endured at the time of her husband's death, Mrs. Parkman determined to found a school to train nurses.

She persuaded the Women's Educational Association, concerned for the plight of Boston's many spinsters, that women trained as nurses would easily find employment.

The Women's Educational Association secured a house at 45 McLean Street, near the Massachusetts General Hospital, to serve as a home for nurses.

Mrs. Parkman then persuaded the trustees of the

hospital to allow pupil nurses to be trained in three wards of the hospital "under a suitable superintendent" to be employed by the ladies.

The first superintendent, a Mrs. Billings, had served as a volunteer nurse during the Civil War. Although she had hastily taken three weeks of training under Sister Helen at Bellevue, Mrs. Billings soon found her task as superintendent too difficult. She resigned.

The second superintendent, the former Mary Phinney of Waltham, had married an *émigré* baron, and as his widow she was known as the Baroness von Olnhausen. A lady of varied talents, she had served as a nurse during the Civil War. She had lectured. She had written articles. But when she took over her duties at the hospital, she soon had the wards in an uproar of mismanagement, and she was asked to resign.

The hospital trustees told Mrs. Parkman that the training school would have to be closed. She was in despair. Someone wrote to Florence Nightingale, begging that she send a Nightingale nurse, to which she replied that for the time being none could be spared for needs outside the Empire.

Finally, Mrs. Parkman prevailed on the trustees to give the little school a year of grace, "if a suitable suitable graduate nurse could be found to take the graduate nurse could be found to take the post of superintendent."

A year ago Linda Richards had declined this post in favor of Bellevue. Now she accepted it, as she wrote to Dr. Dimock, "with fear and trembling."

"But I was determined, quaking as I was, that the school should prove, by the excellence of its nurses, their superiority over nurses who were untrained."

She found the work in the wards poorly organized. The nurses, burdened with housework and cleaning, had little time for their patients. The same nurse seldom saw the same patient twice.

Linda asked a young woman, "Will you tell me, please, what are your duties for the week?"

"On Mondays I wash and iron bandages."

"Do you take care of patients?"

"Not on Mondays, Miss Richards. From half-past five in the morning until long after dark I am kept busy washing, ironing and rolling up bandages."

"I see. And on Tuesdays?"

"On Tuesday I go down to the kitchen, where I work all day."

"Do you tend to the sick at all?"

"Not on Tuesdays. I set up trays. I polish silver. I wash dishes."

"What do you do on Wednesday then? Do you work in wards?"

"Not on that day, Miss Richards; then I serve as the utility nurse. I go from ward to ward with supplies, and I look to the conditions of the closets."

Once a week, serving on night duty, the nurse

took great piles of mending to the ward with her, for even at night the duties of housekeeping seemed to come first. Only one day during the week did she actually serve patients.

Linda went to call on the superintendent of the hospital Dr. Nathan Folsom, a gentleman of breeding, tall, thin, with a carefully rounded, silky gray beard. He regarded her in amazement when she requested that he furnish two scrubwomen for the three wards of the training school.

"Why do you need scrubwomen?" he asked.

"So that the nurses can devote themselves to the work of nursing the patients!"

She reorganized the nursing work completely. She put a nurse in charge of each ward. For this nurse she supplied an assistant.

She insisted that at all times the welfare of the patients must come first, that the nurses must take time to observe the patients. "The power of observation when not inborn must be cultivated. It is inattention that makes us unable to see," she told one young woman.

The nurse who had not known when her patient was dying, stopped Linda in the ward one day. She was not a pupil in the training school, and so she was rather timid in her approach.

"Miss Richards," she asked, "how do you know when a patient is dying?"

"I will tell you how I know. By caring for my patient; by carefully watching and observing the changes that take place from day to day and from hour to hour; by being interested in my patient as a human being entrusted to my care; by being concerned!"

"You mean as if it were someone who belonged to you?" the other one groped as if trying to find the right word to express her awakening feeling, "as if it were someone you loved?"

"Quite so," said Linda. "We always know then."

Linda assigned each pupil nurse to a month of night duty, but not daring to leave the seriously sick patients with nurses who were inexperienced, she often remained in the hospital at night, in order to take care of the grave cases herself.

The pupil nurses lived in the house provided for them on McLean Street. A room for Linda had been rented in a private home on Allen Street a little farther away from the hospital.

When someone became gravely ill in the training school wards at night, a messenger had to be sent all the way to Allen Street, and Linda had to dress hurriedly and rush back to the hospital. This took more than an hour, too much time in case of an emergency.

Often after working all day, Linda stayed on at the hospital all night. Dr. Folsom told her, "No such sacrifice is required of you, Miss Richards."

Linda wished it were true, but aware that he wouldn't understand her deep concern, she replied,

"I will not leave the hospital if there is someone here who might need me!"

Finally the trustees of the hospital grudgingly directed that a room be provided in the hospital for the superintendent of the training school. Linda could now supervise the work of the night nurses much better, and she left instructions that if an emergency arose, she was to be called. If a house doctor had to be summoned, she would be the one to give the order.

The house doctors slept in a dormitory situated on the first floor, near the emergency room of the hospital. For some reason, even in the winter time, they kept their beds swathed with mosquito netting.

When a pupil nurse was sent to call a house doctor, she was supposed to enter the dormitory quietly, awaken only the doctor that was needed, allowing the others to sleep undisturbed.

One night, one of the pupil nurses returned to Linda in tears. The doctors had planted a pile of old shoes and mosquito netting in the middle of the room, so that she fell headlong. Then they lay behind their nettings, hooting and laughing.

This experience was repeated several times, the doctors baiting the pupil nurses because they felt hostile to the training school. "We want none of it," they said.

Finally Linda left orders that no pupil was to go to the house doctors' dormitory; that she was to be wakened to summon the house physician when needed. The first time she was awakened, she went down, threw open the door of the dormitory and called for the particular doctor in such a loud voice that she awakened all the men. She repeated the performance night after night.

Finally they begged her to please send someone to quietly waken the one man that was needed, allowing the others to sleep.

"No more traps?" she asked with a twinkle.

"No more traps!" they promised contritely.

One day Linda asked Dr. Folsom for the use of a storeroom at the end of the corridor on the first floor, across the hall from the quarters of the house physicians.

She ordered this room to be cleaned out. Then she brought in a bed, some blankets and sheets, a papier-mâché mannikin, nursing supplies, bandages, poultices and a bowl of leeches.

In this room on Saturday afternoons she began to give nursing demonstrations to the pupil nurses. She asked the physicians to join the staff of the training school and give medical lectures to the students. They all refused.

In desperation, she met with the lady trustees of the training school one evening, in the little dingy parlor on McLean Street, where above the mantle hung a lithograph showing Florence Nightingale nursing a sick soldier.

Mrs. Parkman, now a frail-looking woman with white hair and a deeply lined face, rose to conduct the meeting. She seemed greatly worried. "We must find some way to provide a medical faculty for our training school," she insisted.

"But if the doctors of our own hospital will not teach our pupils, then what are we to do?" one woman asked. "I am afraid they have beaten us at last. We will have to close the school."

"Not quite yet!" a young woman sprang up. "There must be some other way."

"Perhaps," Linda suggested, "each one of you could call on a friend or a relative who is a physician, and ask him to come and help us."

"Do you mean we should bring in doctors from other hospitals?" The idea was too revolutionary.

"Why not?" Linda asked.

"Hear! Hear!" someone cried. "Let's bring in the doctors from Boston City Hospital. They would come to teach our pupils just to spite the doctors at Massachusetts General."

"Ladies—please, no levity!" Mrs. Parkman urged.

But it was just in this way, and with no nobler motives to impel them, that the doctors from Boston City came to lecture to the pupil nurses at Massachusetts General.

This caused such a furore of comment that one by one the doctors of Massachusetts General, who had refused, offered their services.

Under Linda's direction, the pupil nurses gave good service in the wards. The satisfied patients spoke to their doctors. Some three months after Linda had taken her post as she said, "with fear and trembling," Dr. Folsom summoned her.

"The trustees of the hospital,' he said, "have graciously voted to make one more ward available to the training school."

One of the most noted surgeons in the hospital was Dr. Henry J. Bigelow. His name was well known abroad. However, when it came to the training of nurses, he had always said brusquely, "They need only to know how to keep the hospital clean." Several of his patients had been under the care of pupil nurses, and one, acutely ill after an operation, had been saved by Linda's constant attention day and night.

He stopped Linda one day to thank her. And then, passing his fingers through his fine white beard, a flush of color staining his cheeks and forehead, he said, "Miss Richards, I have changed my opinion. You may send me two of your best pupils each day. I shall take them through the wards with me when I make dressings."

This victory inspired the other doctors. Soon Linda was able to arrange clinical demonstrations for all of the pupils.

"What they see," she declared, "they will know!"

Long before the year of trial had ended for the new school, Dr. Folsom jubilantly informed Linda that the trustees had voted to use pupil nurses in all of the wards.

"I always knew," he declared, "that the training school would prove itself!"

That autumn, the first pupil nurses were graduated. Linda sat on the platform with other dignitaries in one of the lecture halls of the hospital. As the young women rose to receive their diplomas, tears came to her eyes.

She had just heard of the death of her teacher, Dr. Susan Dimock, who had perished at sea when the vessel *Schiller* floundered near the English coast during a storm. Only twenty-eight years old when she died, how greatly she had wrought for the world!

The training school at the Massachusetts General Hospital now grew rapidly. The following winter so many pupils enrolled that they could no longer be housed on McLean Street.

The trustees of the hospital turned over to the training school a building formerly given over to "the foul wards," those for contagious diseases. It was called "the Brick." Remodeled and comfortably furnished, it provided pupil nurses with a residence hall situated right on the hospital grounds.

And now the trustees of the hospital began to look with annoyance at Mrs. Parkman and the other women who had struggled to found the training school as intruders. The doctors spoke proudly of "our training school."

In New York, the same thing was happening. The pioneering group which had founded the training school at Bellevue was being pushed out of sight.

Linda found herself caught more and more in this struggle of transition, feeling loyalties to Mrs. Parkman and yet aware that the nursing school was growing to be more and more a part of the hospital.

How, she wondered, had such matters been settled in England, where the first school to train nurses had been established at St. Thomas' Hospital. She knew that after a four-year course at the Nightingale School at St. Thomas', nurses went out to start schools all over the Empire.

Visitors from abroad were sometimes permitted to come to observe and to study the Nightingale methods as taught at St. Thomas'. Linda wrote to ask if she might be so privileged. So many applied, she knew, that it would be only a miracle if she should be invited.

But the miracle happened, and in the spring of 1877, a letter came from Mrs. Wardroper, the matron of the Nightingale Training School at St. Thomas' Hospital in London, inviting her to be a guest of the school that summer! Linda turned over her work to Mrs. Wohlhaupter with whom she had trained in Roxbury, and who had followed her to serve at Bellevue.

Then at last, on an April morning, Linda Richards stood at the rail of a ship bound from New York to England. She watched the last outlines of the shore disappear into a blue mist on the horizon. She began to think about Florence Night-ingale. She began to wonder what this woman was like who for twenty years had influenced her life.

Chapter XI

"Matron will see you now!"

Linda followed the probationer in the brown frock and the flickering white apron as she passed swiftly down the long, gleaming hallways of St. Thomas' Hospital.

The new buildings of the hospital, erected recently on the Albert Embankment in Lambeth, overlooking the Thames, framed a view of the lacy towers of Parliament. And as Linda passed an open window, from across the river she could hear the mellow echoing of Big Ben.

The probationer opened a heavy mahogany door respectfully, then stepped back, saying with the awe that one would use before majesty, "Mrs. Wardroper, may I present Miss Richards?"

Linda found herself in the presence of a tiny, erect old woman dressed in rustling black silk, on her head a beautiful lace cap with ribbons that streamed in back to her waistline. She sat at an ornate desk writing, her hands encased in tight, black kid gloves.

Greeting Linda with gracious formality, she said, "We are pleased to receive America's first trained nurse." Linda sensed that Mrs. Wardroper spoke both for Miss Nightingale and herself.

For twenty years, Miss Nightingale, the "lady-in-chief" of the hospital, had been an invalid in her London flat. Yet from her couch with numerous notes sent every day, she directed the work of the training school.

"It has been arranged," Mrs. Wardroper told Linda, "that you shall live in the nurses' home on the hospital grounds. You'll wear a Nightingale uniform, and for one week at a time you may work in each of the eight wards of the training school."

Linda expressed her deep gratitude and asked if she might convey to Miss Nightingale a report in person as to the state of Nightingale nursing in America.

"Miss Nightingale sees no visitors!"

Linda went away disappointed, but she could not give up hope. A few days later, she moved into the charming room provided for her at the nurses' home, furnished like the most gracious English dwelling.

The home sister, Miss Crossland, a dark-haired lady of distinguished bearing, invited Linda to sit beside her at the head table in the lovely dining room, where a fire glowed on the hearth, and on the open fender a teakettle bubbled and sang.

As the nurses came in to dinner, some took

dainty teapots from the closet and filled them at the hearth, brewing their own cups of tea. Others sat at a table, where a presiding nurse poured tumblers of beer out of a tall pitcher.

Some of the nurses were introduced to Linda as "Miss" and some as "Nurse." All wore the same uniform. Linda asked Miss Crossland why they were addressed differently.

"A lady probationer is called 'Miss,' and a nurse probationer is called 'Nurse.' "

"What," Linda asked, "is the difference?"

"A lady probationer," Miss Crossland explained, "is a lady; that is, she comes from the upper classes; she is better educated. She pays a fee to attend the school. And when she is graduated she will be sent out to found a school to train nurses."

"And a nurse probationer?"

"A nurse probationer is a young lady from the lower classes. She has had less education. She cannot pay a fee, of course. Instead she receives an allowance while at school."

"And when she is graduated?"

"She remains a nurse. Sometimes a lady and her personal maid will both enroll at the school at the same time. They receive the same training except that the better-educated woman will eventually teach others."

"In America," Linda replied thoughtfully, "a nurse can become a teacher in only one way."

"How is that?"

"By doing her work so well," Linda answered, "that she has the right to direct others!"

Miss Crossland explained calmly, "Our ways are different. When class distinctions disappear in this country, they will also disappear from this school."

"Does Miss Nightingale favor class distinctions?" Linda asked.

"She did not ask the wounded of the Crimean War to which class they belonged!" was Miss Crossland's reply.

The next day, Linda put on a Nightingale uniform and took her place with the other probationers. She found the hospital work beautifully organized. The guiding hand of the lady-in-chief, as the absent Miss Nightingale was called, could be felt everywhere, the most meticulous and exacting care being given to the patients.

Linda became acquainted with the many curious customs of the hospital. The head nurse in each ward was known as "Sister." She was called not by her given name, but by the name of her ward. Some of the wards were named for members of the royal family, some for the type of cases treated. There was a Sister Albert and a Sister Victoria. The sister in charge of the eye ward where ophthalmic cases were treated was known as Sister Ophthalmia.

The probationers were given classroom training for a year. This consisted of lectures and clinical demonstrations by the hospital physicians, and bedside instruction by head nurses responsible to Mrs. Wardroper, who in turn took orders from Miss Nightingale.

The relationship of these two women was quite remarkable. Each respected the special abilities of the other. The two worked as one.

When Miss Nightingale returned a heroine from the Crimean War a grateful nation raised a fund to honor her. This fund, a sum of fifty thousand pounds, was set aside to start a hospital school to train nurses. But Florence Nightingale had become an invalid during the war. She could not conduct the work of the school in person. She chose St. Thomas' Hospital as the site of the school and Mrs. Wardroper as the matron.

This tiny gentlwoman, left a widow at the age of forty-two, had gone to work at old St. Thomas' in the days when the nurses were drunken charwomen, and all kinds of horror existed in the wards.

She had brought order, cleanliness and good management to the wards with the same quiet self-assurance with which she had once managed her own gracious home.

She carried out the orders of Miss Nightingale without fume or fuss, and like anyone in command of herself, she expected implicit obedience from others. She was never known to raise her voice above a whisper, yet her appearance struck awe. She never said, "I direct." She always said, "It is the wish of our lady-in-chief!"

Each probationer, at the end of her training,

took a rigorous examination. Mrs. Wardroper examined the answers and then Miss Nightingale, to whom all examination questions were forwarded.

The graduate nurse then remained to work in the hospital for three more years under supervision. At the end of that time she was assigned to a post outside by Miss Nightingale. She might be sent to any part of the United Kingdom, or to the most distant corner of the Empire. Wherever she was sent, she went.

Lucy Osburn, a Nightingale nurse, had been sent to found a training school in the hospital in Sydney, Australia. From this hospital, a graduate had gone on to become the first matron of the hospital in Melbourne.

In this way, from St. Thomas' Hospital there stretched out a web of service reaching to all parts of the world. A frail, sick woman, never seen in the hospital, commanded the lives of hundreds of women who went out to serve.

Linda asked Miss Crossland one day, "Is it really impossible to see Miss Nightingale? Does she receive no one?"

"Not even royalty!" Miss Crossland answered.

Regretting that she could not be received, Linda had made notes on the state of American nursing, which she sent on to Miss Nightingale. She went on to tell about the two training schools she set up in America that used the Nightingale methods; one at Bellevue Hospital and the other at Massachusetts General.

"With the latter I have been especially concerned, working for three years as superintendent of the training school where a two-year course is now given to the pupil nurses."

Linda told of the opposition she had encountered in starting the work of this school, of the type of pupils taught, "who are generally young women of good education and good breeding, coming from all classes, as is the custom in our country.

"We do not command the lives of the nurses after they have graduated," she wrote, "but we aim to breed a spirit of *esprit de corps* and loyalty to the hospital."

Linda sent off this letter, expecting she might receive merely a polite note of acknowledgment perhaps from Miss Nightingale's secretary. She was amazed to receive an invitation to luncheon, written by Florence Nightingale herself.

Linda nervously mounted the stone steps at South Street. Her knees shook. An impassive footman took her shawl in a little reception hall and then led her upstairs to Miss Nightingale's sitting room.

Linda was ushered into the presence of a lady of about sixty, lying on a couch, her head slightly raised on a sapphire pillow.

She was dressed all in black, with a bit of lace pinned to her dark hair, which was parted in the

116

center and drawn down smoothly at either side of her face.

She had keen blue eyes, and an extraordinarily sweet expression, combining somehow the impressions of saint, general and great lady!

She held out her hand. "Take a seat my dear," she said in a very kind voice. "As you can see, I cannot rise to receive you. I have been troubled with rheumatism of the spine which sometimes keeps me attached to this couch."

A worktable heaped with papers stood beside her. The sitting room was lined on all sides from ceiling to floor with books, papers and reports.

"I have read with great care the notes you sent me about your nursing work in America. We were often importuned to send Nightingale nurses to your country. But first we had to serve the needs of the Empire.

"Now I see that you have developed the work in quite your own way. And if you have learned from us, I believe that in turn we can learn from you."

She asked Linda many penetrating questions about the training given at the New England Hospital, at Bellevue and at Massachusetts General.

"I regretted greatly that I could not see Dr. Susan Dimock when she visited here, or Dr. Gill Wylie of Bellevue.

"As you know, I have been greatly concerned to see better care given to the sick and to the wounded in the British army. At last we have a training school to instruct army nurses.

"And for years I have been occupied with the lack of medical attention in India where, due to the customs of *purdah,* a physician cannot even come near a woman patient, and thousands die each year without care."

Miss Nightingale asked Linda about the state of workhouse nursing in America.

"We send our indigent sick to city hospitals."

"And are these well managed?" Miss Nightingale asked.

Linda told of her experiences as a ward maid at the Boston City Hospital. She told about the system of night watchers. She told about the death of a boy at night alone and unattended.

"Why did you decide to become a nurse?" Miss Nightingale asked.

"I read a book which moved me greatly. It was called *Una and Her Paupers.*"

"Ah," Miss Nightingale sighed, "the story of Agnes Jones. She was one of our saints!"

The footman brought in luncheon which was served on a silver tray near the couch. Linda was scarcely aware of what was put on her plate. The footman offered a second serving.

"My dear," Miss Nightingale chided, "cook will be disappointed. I asked her to prepare one of her very best dishes for the nurse from America."

Before Linda left, Miss Nightingale advised her to go and work for a month if possible at the

King's College Hospital, where the nursing work was done by the Sisters of St. John, an Anglican order.

"There you will learn the beauties of obedience."

And if Linda could get to Scotland, the lady-in-chief recommended, "by all means go to observe at the Royal Infirmary in Edinburgh, where Miss Pringle, one of our finest nurses, is the matron. You will find her a little general."

As Linda rose to leave, Miss Nightingale took her hand and with a warm smile she said, "I have enjoyed your visit, my chick, come back to see me again before you leave England."

Linda did not know if she walked back to the nurses home or floated back! When the nurses crowded around her to ask her impression, she could only say, choking back tears of happiness, "Wonderful! Wonderful!"

She went, as Miss Nightingale had suggested, to ask permission to spend a month working in the wards at King's College Hospital. Miss Crossland accompanied her. Linda refused to use Miss Nightingale's name.

The Mother Superior of the hospital, a grave lady dressed in dark, nunlike robes, a crucifix hanging at her side, told Linda, "Regretfully, only members of our order may work in the wards. But you may come and make notes whenever you wish."

Linda could not help writing Miss Nightingale

of her disappointment. Some days later, returning to make notes at the hospital, she was greeted by a little sister who seemed very excited.

"The Mother Superior has reconsidered. She asks me to tell you, Miss Richards, that you have been invited to work in the wards!"

At first Linda could not understand why this had happened. Then she learned that the Mother Superior and Miss Nightingale had served together in the Crimea. And a note from the lady-in-chief had worked magic!

Linda lived in the nurses home provided for the lady probationers. She wore their uniform, a black alpaca dress, a brown linen apron and a white linen cap with a turned-back ruffle, rather like a bonnet, which tied with an organdy bow under the chin.

A sister presided over the home where the probationers lived. She accompanied them to and from the hospital where they took their meals. "Both on arriving in the morning and on leaving at night," Linda wrote to Miss Crossland, "the roll is called and the name of each probationer is checked off. If a nurse has a visitor, the visitor is received in the reception room, where Sister Ami's door always stands open."

The probationers were given no time off, except to go to chapel in the morning and to church on Sunday. They all took the vow of implicit obedience.

One day Linda broke a rule without knowing

120

that she did so. In a hurry to go from the second to the first floor of the hospital, she used the front stairs.

Later, dignified Sister Ami said to her in the kindest way possible, "You broke a rule this morning, which I am sure you would not have done, if you had known."

"Indeed not, Sister Ami. Please tell me what I did that was wrong."

"You used the front stairs, which are to be used only by the doctors!"

Linda found the patients treated kindly, the work of the hospital orderly and strangely unhurried. "Here there is not the hurry and rush that one usually sees," she wrote to Miss Crossland.

"The work is always done in season. The wards are all in order at the proper time. Every nurse seems to know and do her own duty, and that with few words. No one assumes the duties or responsibilities of another.

"For instance," Linda went on to say, "in the absence of the ward sister, the only answer given to a visiting doctor concerning a patient will be, 'Sister will be here directly.' "

Linda found the atmosphere of the hospital homelike. At each end of the ward, there was a huge fireplace, where a fire was kept brightly glowing. At night, potatoes were boiled in a pot hung before the ward fire, so that they could be served hot to the ward patients. A young probationer did this work and then went from bed to bed serving the hot potatoes in their jackets.

Each patient who came to the hospital brought his own teapot, cup, saucer, plate and utensils. These were kept in a little locker by his bed, and the nurse who washed the dishes, returned them to his locker after each meal.

At five in the morning, the night nurses gave bread, butter and tea to all the patients. Two night nurses were assigned to each ward. They took their meals at midnight, on opposite sides of the ward, never visiting together.

The hospital was immaculate from attic to cellar. The infectious cases were nursed in the general wards. Linda nursed a boy with scarlet fever and a man sick with typhoid, both in the same room. No ill effects seemed to result, which surprised Linda very much.

A spirit of calm pervaded the hospital. The nurses worked twice as hard as American nurses, yet never complained of their work or of the discipline. "An everpresent cheerfulness seems to prevail," Linda confided in a letter to Miss Nightingale, "which is a very beautiful feature of the sisters' religion."

Years later Linda was to say, "Rules have never seemed either irksome or out of place since I learned from the sisters to obey cheerfully and unquestioningly."

She went on to Scotland, arriving in Edinburgh

on an August afternoon, when the city was darkened by a driving rainstorm.

She caught only brief glimpses of the narrow streets with brick houses on either side. Then after a short drive, the cab stopped before a group of old gray stone buildings crowded together behind an ivy-covered enclosure.

The hospital buildings, connected by numerous passages, were very old, the ceilings low, the wards crowded. But they were spotlessly clean, and looked "so cozy." At the end of each ward glowed a bright fire, where the teakettle boiled and some of the recovering patients gathered to chat.

Linda found Miss Pringle to be as Miss Nightingale had described her, "a little general," but what a warm, kindly and loving general she proved to be.

She allowed the men patients to smoke for an hour each day, "at which time, in the men's wards, one can hardly see across the room," Linda wrote in her notes.

Because there were not enough beds to go around, as soon as a patient felt better, he left his bed to accept a shakedown, a clean ticking filled with straw, placed on the floor.

One morning, in a little side room, Linda came upon an old man sleeping on a shakedown. In his arms he held another patient, a little boy of about two. The baby slept peacefully cuddled against the old man's grizzled beard.

"I see you had a bedfellow last night," Linda said smiling.

"Aye," he responded with a twinkle, "I get on fine with the bairnies!"

In this crowded, old-fashioned hospital, a great surgeon had made a great discovery. Joseph Lister had found out that germs could cause surgical infection. He had gone to lecture at King's College Hospital.

Linda went to the Sunday morning clinics held by his assistant, Dr. Joseph Bell, who demonstrated that surgical wounds could be made to heal without the long, exhausting suppuration which had once been thought necessary.

Linda shuddered when she recalled how she used to wash out bandages from one patient to use on another; how the doctors used to go from bed to bed, using the same sponge to dip out one wound after another.

In September, she left Edinburgh, and before returning to America, she went to visit Florence Nightingale at her country home, Lea Hurst. Miss Nightingale had gone there to visit her aged mother.

Once more Linda found Miss Nightingale on a couch, but as before, eager, enthusiastic, interested in everything that pertained to nursing. She listened as Linda told of the many impressions she had received.

"Our work," said Miss Nightingale, "must never

become merely a profession. It must always remain a calling."

On board ship, Linda received a letter from Miss Nightingale. "May you outstrip us," she wrote, "so that we in turn may outstrip you!"

Chapter XII

Some six months later, on a cold day in January, Linda passed through the iron gates of the Boston City Hospital, where once she had worked briefly as a ward maid.

She went to the reception room outside the superintendent's office, and Dr. Edward Cowles, who had recently taken that post, came out smiling to greet her.

"Well, Miss Richards," he said, "Have you come to accept my offer?" He was a handsome man with graying side whiskers. In his eyes there was the look of a reformer, and he was known for his liberal ideas.

"I am quite ready," she answered.

"I must warn you," he said, "that the doctors on the staff are not friendly to the work for which I have employed you. They do not want a school to train nurses here."

"That," replied Linda with a rueful smile, "is not at all a new situation for me."

Together they went down the hallway to the

small office which had been provided for Linda as matron of the hospital and superintendent of the training school.

Linda drew up the curriculum for the school. "We shall teach the dressing of blisters, burns, sores and wounds," she wrote, "the applying of fomentations, poultices and leeches.

"Massaging and bandaging shall be taught. Nurses will be trained to observe their patients accurately in regard to pulse, temperatures and all other changes."

As Linda passed through the wards one day, she stopped to ask a nurse about the condition of a patient who had been very ill for some time.

"He is better," the nurse reported.

"How do you know?" Linda asked.

"Oh, he has not called me for over an hour."

Linda went at once to the patient's bed, where she found him in a coma. She returned to the nurse. "Didn't you realize," she said sternly, "that the patient did not call you because he was too weak to speak?"

In the dining room where Linda took her meals with the staff physicians, she indignantly told this story. "Can we put the lives of people into the hands of those who are not trained?" No one at the table answered.

Linda called a meeting of all the untrained women working in the hospital. She told each one that she would be credited with a year of training, if she would enroll in the school.

"The day will come," Linda warned, "when no nurse will be able to work unless she has been trained."

Not one of the women present rose to enroll. Then down the hallway came the sound of waddling footsteps, and stout Rosa McCormick whom Linda remembered, came puffing into the room.

"Am I too late?" she cried. "Thirteen years ago, I was the first nurse hired when this hospital opened. I want to be the first nurse to enroll in the training school."

Inspired by Rosa's example, sixteen other women enrolled in the course. Linda secured three graduate nurses to help her, one from the New England Hospital where she had trained, and two from Bellevue.

She eliminated the old system of night watchers. She hired scrubwomen to do the heavy cleaning in the wards. She assigned some of the pupil nurses to day duty and some to night duty. She set up the system of recordkeeping which she had originated at Bellevue.

All these changes were greeted with disapproval by the house doctors. She told Dr. Cowles one day, "Looks of bare tolerance greet me on my rounds, and I am made to feel that my suggestions are an interference." He made no reply, only sighed and shook his head.

She began a letter one night. "Pardon me, dear Miss Nightingale," she wrote, "for taking the liberty to trouble you." She thought of all the difficulties she would like to confide. Instead she wrote, "I live on my days at St. Thomas' and at the Royal Infirmary. Very often when I am very weary I think of those days, and it rests me."

Linda designed a uniform for the pupil nurses, a gray and white dress to be worn with a white apron, and a stiff white cap with a fluted edging.

On May 1, 1878, the training school opened officially, with an enrollment of over sixty pupils. Some of the hospital nurses who had enrolled in the course had difficulty in passing the quizzes. The trustees felt that they should not be dropped because of their loyalty to the hospital.

Linda rose to state her views. "Gentlemen, I was told by Miss Nightingale that the finest nurse to serve in the Crimea was a Mrs. Roberts, who was so skilled in the care of the sick that she could have taught even the surgeons.

"Yet the time came when it was Miss Nightingale's painful duty to tell Mrs. Roberts that she could not be admitted to the Nightingale Training School, because she could not read and write!"

"And do you consider that just and fair, Miss Richards?" one of the trustees asked.

"I consider it just to the cause of nursing since it established the principle that no one can train as a nurse who is not educated!"

Of the seventeen hospital nurses who had enrolled in the course, eleven were dropped because they could not read and write. Rosa McCormick was not one of these. On May 1, 1879, she received her diploma.

The doctors at last ceased their opposition to the training school. They welcomed the disciplined pupil nurses, and more pupils enrolled in the school.

They slept in little rooms between the wards. These rooms were so crowded that the girls sometimes had to dress on their beds. There was no room on the floor for them to stand up!

They had no chairs to sit on, no place where they could receive visitors. They could not get away from the sights and sounds of the hospital, not even for an hour.

"Our students cannot do good work," Linda complained to the trustees, "if they have to live under such conditions."

The trustees made appeals to the city commissioners for funds to build a home for nurses on the hospital grounds. The commissioners put the matter aside, again and again.

Dr. Cowles resigned as superintendent of the hospital to become director of the McLean Hospital in Waverly, an institution long known for its outstanding care of the mentally ill.

"These are the most neglected patients of all," he told Linda, "and someday they, too, shall be given proper care by trained nurses."

But Linda, concerned with the dream of a proper home for her students, scarcely listened. She went on appealing to the trustees and the city commissioners.

The new superintendent of the hospital Dr. George Rowe, a judicious-looking man, peered at Linda through his gold-rimmed spectacles.

"It will take time to secure an appropriation from the city," he said calmly. "We will have to interest the newspapers. We will have to educate the public. And then in time, the City Council, pushed from all sides, may vote us part of the sum needed."

"That may take years!" Linda cried.

"Miss Richards, it always does when you ask for public funds."

In August, Linda fell ill with a fever, followed by an infection of the lungs. She went to Foxboro to rest. Two years passed before she could return to take up her work again at the hospital. She found the students still living in the same crowded quarters.

That autumn, Dr. Rowe wrote in his annual report, "We find in the sixth year of the training school that the City Coucil still refuses to make us an appropriation so that our nurses may be assured of healthful living quarters.

"Other departments of the city," he accused, "are well housed and liberally maintained. Our nurses are our finest product!"

Two more years passed with appeal after appeal to the trustees, the commissioners, to the City Council. Finally, in 1883, the Council voted a fund of forty thousand dollars for the building of a nurses home on the hospital grounds. Linda wept with joy!

For two years, she pored over the plans and watched the new four-story building of red brick as it rose stone by stone.

She fought for comfortably furnished rooms, wide porches, spacious parlors, open fireplaces, a setting of charm and graciousness which could help to shape lives.

She dreamed over every sofa, every table, every curtain, as if homeless all her life, she were furnishing her own home at last. She sought the gift of a grand piano and soft carpets and walls of books.

The new home was located at the edge of the hospital grounds, and it was separated from the hospital by a high hedge fence, in which there was a little locked gate.

She provided each nurse with a key to this gate, saying, "This is the key to your own home!" Finally the happy day of moving came, and then the dedication ceremonies.

In the autumn of 1885, the new nurses home was dedicated with a public reception held in the beautiful double parlors. Many distinguished guests came, and visitors from afar who were interested in nursing.

It might have been at this time that Linda met Dr. John C. Berry, a young medical missionary who had done outstanding work in Japan, and who spoke with fervor of starting a school in that country to train nurses.

"In that far-off country?" Linda asked.

"Miss Richards, you could serve no greater purpose!"

This idea, so extraordinary, kept pressing in her mind. "I found it facing me at every turn," she wrote. "Finally, as an act of seeming duty, I went to the rooms of the American Board in Boston and offered my services."

She hoped never to hear of the matter again. "It was with something like surprise that in August, 1885, I received word that I had been appointed."

She left in December for Japan. She had signed a contract to remain for five years. On the way to San Francisco by train, she still could not understand what had happened to her, or why she was going!

Chapter XIII

At midnight, Linda stood at the rail, watching with the other passengers for a glimpse of the approaching shores of Japan.

For a month the ship had been steaming over the endless Pacific. For over two weeks they had seen no other vessel. That afternoon they had passed through a storm and a gale.

Now the sea lay like velvet, touched here and there by flecks of moonlight. On the horizon floated a bank of milky white clouds veiled by a mysterious mist like a silvery emanation.

"You may see it at almost any moment," one of the women passengers told Linda eagerly. "Those who catch a glimpse of the peak of Fujiyama will have good fortune during their stay in Japan."

"Do you believe this legend?" Linda asked.

"Everyone believes the legend. The Japanese worship this mountain, perfect in shape, which rises two miles high from the plains of Tokyo. They call it 'the honorable mountain!' "

As the woman spoke someone cried in great

excitement, "There, there, over there!" Everyone crowded to the rail.

Almost crushed by the people pushing behind her, Linda saw on the horizon the veil of mist parting, and for an instant she thought that she glimpsed an opalescent peak swimming among the snowy clouds.

"Fujiyama! Fujiyama!"

But the next moment she was not certain of what she had seen. "I shall never know," she said to the woman beside her, "Whether I shall have good fortune or not in Japan."

The next morning she went on deck early. The ship had stopped about a mile and a half from the harbor of Yokohama. In the distance she saw fishing nets spread out in all directions, like a huge spider web covering the whole bay.

Round the ship, hundreds of natives had gathered in flat-bottomed boats, and shoving their boats alongside, they tried violently to get on board, while the ship's officers with equal effort pushed them off.

"What is happening?" Linda asked of the woman who had spoken to her the evening before. This woman, the wife of an import merchant, returning to join her husband in Japan, seemed to know all the native customs. She watched the commotion quite undisturbed.

"The ship has to wait here for the ship's launch to come out to take the passengers off. Sometimes a passenger may be in a great hurry. He may not want to wait, and he may hire a native boatman."

Linda looked out with amazement as the officers pushed the boatmen away from the sides of the ship with long poles, often hitting them on the head or arms.

"And all these men come out here hoping to make a few pennies by rowing one passenger across the harbor to the docks?"

The merchant's wife, a small woman dressed in a tight basque, an expensive shawl on her shoulders, said with some disdain, "You forget that this is Japan!"

The launch finally appeared. The boatmen, kneeling in their flat-bottomed boats, rowed away. The passengers were taken to the docks.

There a Japanese customs official, who could speak a few words of English, gave Linda directions for reaching Kyoto. There was no railroad so she had to take a coastal steamer to Kobe, which lay on the inland sea between two islands, and from there a short train ride to reach the ancient capital of the Mikados.

The steamer for Kobe did not leave until the next day at dawn. Dr. Berry had arranged that Linda stay in Yokohama with a missionary couple who lived on "the Cliff." Since Commodore Perry had first come to Yokohama in 1854, leaving behind him an emissary who chose to live on this height, all families of foreigners had dwelt there, either in rented Japanese dwellings, or if they could afford to do so, in their own Western-style houses.

Linda took a jinrikisha to "the Cliff." On shipboard, she had been surprised to learn that this vehicle which she had thought of as Japanese had been invented by an American missionary in Japan. His wife became an invalid and he devised a kind of a two-wheeled cart, using the wheels of a baby buggy. A buggy-maker in Worcester, Massachusetts, then began to manufacture these two-wheeled carts, which soon took the place of the palanquins in which Japanese passengers had been carried on the shoulders of coolies.

Linda looked out from the swaying jinrikisha as her coolie ran without stopping through the crowded streets, past strangely fragile little dwellings built on stilts, past shops with wares open to the sidewalks, and through crowds of men, kimono-clad women and children clattering on wooden clogs. Their thin singsong language had no more meaning to her than the rustling of paper. She wondered with despair if she could ever learn the meaning of such a language.

When the runner reached the foot of "the Cliff," a high green embankment crowned at the top with little walled houses, he stopped in the shafts and pointing upward said, "Takawok!"

He repeated this remark several times, each time pointing upward. "Takawok! Takawok!" Finally Linda realized with a shock that he was saying "Take a walk."

She dismounted. He politely led the way on foot, up a steep path. She had to sit down twice to rest. Finally they reached the dwelling of the missionary couple.

"We have not yet been able to build our own Western home," the missionary's wife explained. She was a little, birdlike woman, with brown hair elaborately dressed. "Your greatest struggle in this country will be with corsets," she told Linda.

"How so?" Linda asked, trying not to look startled.

"Just wait until you have to kneel on a mat for an hour or two, and you have to bow a dozen times, touching your forehead to the ground!

"They say that the apostle James spent so much time in prayer that his knees became calloused like those of a camel whose natural position it is to kneel.

"Well," she chattered on loquaciously, "we who come to Japan soon find that our great longing is for a chair or a bench to sit upon. Believe me, my knees are like those of a camel."

In the little Japanese dwelling there were no chairs; in fact, there was no furniture at all in the tiny rooms, which had paper walls and beautifully polished floors. All the rooms looked alike. In each, a vase or a wall hanging was the only decoration.

The two women knelt on the floor, warming their hands over a *hibachi,* a little round pot filled with glowing charcoal. It was a clear, bright January day. During the hours of sunlight, it had been quite warm. But now a cold wind blew from the harbor. It penetrated the thin walls.

"How do the Japanese people keep warm?" Linda asked with a shiver.

The missionary's wife began to laugh. "By soaking in hot water."

She clapped her hands and a maid appeared. She bowed low when the little, birdlike woman gave her directions and pointed to Linda.

Half an hour later, the maid came back with a cotton kimono, which she offered to Linda, with many polite bows and gestures.

"What she saying?" Linda asked.

"That as an honored guest of the house, you shall be the first to enter the bath. My husband will follow you, then I, then each of the servants in turn."

"All in the same water?" Linda asked, horrified.

Her hostess laughed. "This is Japan."

Linda was taken to a room beyond the kitchen, in which there stood the strangest tub she had ever seen in her life. It was square like a well, but high and narrow, not long enough for a person to lie down in. It was evident that the bather, with his knees drawn up, would have to squat in the tub which was so deep that the water would reach beyond the shoulder.

The tub was covered on the outside with closely fitted wooden slats, vertical in arrangement, rather like a fence. Into the side of this very strange bathtub was built something that looked like a little brick stove, from which smoke issued.

Linda soon learned the purpose of this heating device. The tub was filled with steaming hot buckets of water which then could be kept at a constant temperature.

The maid motioned to Linda that she should wash herself with a basin of warm water and soap before she entered the tub. A bath was evidently not for cleansing but for keeping warm.

Linda soaked for an hour in the tub, and came out as her hostess had told her she would, feeling warm and not mindful of the chill in the house.

Many storekeepers, the missionary's wife told her, had a tub behind the counter. And during the day, in their chilly little shops, they got into the tub to soak. It was their only way to get warm.

"And what happens if a customer comes in?" Linda asked.

"Oh, then the shopkeeper jumps streaming out of the tub to wait on him. And then he jumps in again to warm himself once more, until the next customer arrives!"

She evidently enjoyed telling Linda these unusual details, and she went on in a whispering voice, until her husband, the missionary, arrived. He had been holding an evening meeting in the Japanese Christian church which had been opened in Yokohama a few years before.

He was a tall, bald man with a freckled forehead

and a thin fringe of reddish hair. He told Linda that in Kyoto it would be her privilege to work with two great men—Dr. Joseph Neesima, the Japanese president of Doshisha University, the first college founded to spread Western learning; and with Dr. John C. Berry, a medical missionary beloved by thousands in Japan.

That night Linda slept on a Japanese bed, a wadding taken out of the wall and put down on the floor, under her head a little pillow filled with oats. The pillow was shaped rather like a rolling pin. She lay covered with two huge silken kimonos which kept sliding off her feet.

Long before dawn she was awakened by the maid who brought her tea, and told her with signals that the missionary and his wife were waiting to take her to the steamer. They went with her to the wharf. There she embarked on one of the countless small, flat-bottomed boats, a coolie rowing her silently over the still, dark waters to the steamer lying a mile away in the bay.

The steamer was crowded with men, women and children kneeling on deck, and on every foot of space in the hold. Linda had a first-class ticket and was allowed to kneel on a shelf, two feet off the floor.

The journey from Yokohama to Kobe took twenty-four hours. Her back ached, her knees felt numb. She felt ill from eating a strange dish of salty fish flakes served on rice. She longed with all her heart for a chair and a cup of coffee.

The next morning, the steamer reached Kobe, a city of low, flat houses, the streets filled with crowds of people in gray kimonos, their clogs echoing on the macadam roads.

She found the wooden station and took a rattling train which an official, communicating in sign language, told her was bound for Kyoto.

The train had no seats, only long wooden shelves at either side of each car, on which the passengers kneeled. A peasant woman nursed a baby, taking sidelong glances at Linda. A fat gentleman in a quilted kimono dozed, his hands folded in the sleeves of his kimono.

Frequently the train stopped and boys came in selling little straw baskets of hot rice and containers filled with slivers of fish cooked in a peculiar brown sauce.

Linda ate some of the rice with a spoon which she had brought with her in her handbag. The Japanese passengers tried not to stare, but she could see that from time to time they stole sidelong glances.

The train finally arrived in Kyoto, a beautiful city of temples and pagodas, lovely gardens and parks. Linda rode in a jinrikisha past the high walls surrounding the old imperial palaces, from which the Mikados had been removed after the struggle with the feudal lords which took place not long after Perry's visit to Japan.

On Temple Street, not far from Doshisha University built near the now vacant palaces, Linda got off before a new Western-style residence with glass windows instead of paper screens.

There in a parlor furnished with tables, sofas, and armchairs, where a carpet lay on the floor and pictures hung on the wall, she was greeted by Mrs. Berry, the wife of the medical missionary.

Dr. Berry, who lectured on physiology at the University was not at home. Mrs. Berry, a delicate little lady with fine features and a sweet New England voice, kissed Linda. There were tears in her eyes.

"Having a visitor from America is almost like going home. I have hundreds of questions to ask you. But first I have a surprise for you. Sit down, please, in that big armchair."

With a sigh Linda sank into the deep, soft chair.

"Oh, I know what it means to sit in an armchair when your back feels as if it were breaking!" the little lady told her. "And what it means to have a soft bed to lie upon when you have slept on the floor. It took us years, but at last we have brought our own things from America, and we can live as we did at home."

She clapped her hands and a little Japanese maid came in. Mrs. Berry spoke to her in quick, singsong Japanese. The maid smiled and withdrew, returning with a tray on which stood a steaming pitcher of coffee and thin slices of toast with butter.

"Oh," Linda's hands trembled as she reached for the coffee.

"That's the surprise," her hostess said. "The Japanese do not milk their cows. They use them only as beasts of burden. The milk and the butter were brought over from America in tins. It's a great luxury when a ship arrives and we can have a fresh supply."

Linda drank the coffee and ate the toast on which the butter seemed a little rancid. But to her it tasted delicious.

"Tell me," she said to Mrs. Berry, "how long does it take to learn the Japanese language?"

"Did you catch a glimpse of Fujiyama when you approached the shores of Japan?"

"I am not quite certain, but it may be that I did."

"Well, in that case," said Mrs. Berry with a twinkle, "it will take you only three years."

Chapter XIV

Linda knelt on a cushion by a small, low table on which there lay a pencil and notebook. Her lips moved as she tried to say over and over again the Japanese phrases that bewildered her.

The paper door slid open noiselessly, and a pretty girl in a gray silk kimono bowed so low to the floor that the delicate bone pins in her lacquered hair made a clicking sound on the polished wood. She bowed again and again.

"I am Ito San," she said in halting English. "I have been sent from the Doshisha School to humbly teach our language to the Honorable One who will train us to be nurses."

For nine months, Linda had been studying Japanese, first with a man teacher, then in the town of Okayama, some seventy miles from Kyoto, with a missionary versed in instruction. Now she had returned to Kyoto, where shortly she hoped to start training the five young women from the Mission School, who had come to undertake their education as nurses. Ito San was to be one of these students.

Linda knew the personal story of this pretty girl, who had been sent away by her husband because she wanted to study the religion which the foreigners had brought from overseas, and which the Buddhist and the Shinto priests condemned as unholy.

Ito San did not want to leave her handsome and noble husband whom she loved. But when her mother-in-law said that one who entertains the new ideas is not welcome in the house, then her husband wrote out on a piece of paper the words which meant that Ito San was no longer his wife, that by his wish she had been divorced.

For three years Ito San had been studying English in the preparatory school of the Doshisha University. This college, which began with eight pupils ten years ago, now had almost five hundred students.

It was the first college in Japan which allowed both men and women to become students. It was founded and administered by Joseph Neesima, a remarkable man, a Japanese of noble birth once in the service of a prince. At the risk of his life, he ran away from his country to study in America.

Then returning to his native land, he founded in Kyoto, the ancient capital of the Mikados and the great center of the Buddhist religion, a college to teach the new Western learning.

In connection with this college, he had been

trying to establish a medical school. The medical missionary Dr. John Cutting Berry, who gave lectures on physiology and anatomy at the college, had been working day and night to raise money.

But not enough money had been raised for the medical school, which finally was abandoned. Now Dr. Berry was trying to raise money to build a small hospital on the grounds of the university, to start a school there to teach nurses.

There had been great opposition among the Japanese people to this plan. A woman should stay at home, they believed. It was not fit that she should go out to nurse strangers. It would not be proper! One nurses only in the bosom of the family, those to whom one is related. One does not touch the bodies of other persons.

Struggling with the complexities of the Japanese language and waiting long months to start her work of teaching, Linda became impatient.

She told both Dr. Berry and President Neesima that it would be wasting time to wait until they had the means to put up a proper building in which to set up a hospital. "Why can't we start now in the little Mission House where I live?"

In this dwelling with paper walls, a large room at the front had been made into a dispensary for Berry *Sensei,* or "master," as the Japanese patients called the tall, bearded medical missionary, whose methods brought them better cures than the "holy papers" they pasted on their bodies to charm away the evil spirits of sickness.

On the upper floor, three small rooms had been set aside for patients, and one room for Linda and a missionary teacher Miss Gardiner, who was temporarily staying at the Mission House. Into two little rooms behind the kitchen, the five pupil nurses would be crowded.

Linda would be in charge of the household. She wanted to learn the proper words for instructing the cook who would prepare meals for the patients when they came.

She began her lesson with Ito San. "I want to learn the proper way to say the word *rice*," she said.

Ito San touched her forehead to the floor. This was a habit as natural as breath to her. And Linda did not try to correct her.

"Of which kind of rice shall we speak, O Honorable One?" the little interpreter asked.

Linda was bewildered. "I wish merly to speak of rice."

"For cooking," Ito San asked politely, "for eating, for growing, for serving to yourself O Honorable One, or to a child, or to an honored guest?"

Linda tried not to show her bewilderment. "Is not *ine* the word for rice?" she asked. "The other day I called in the maid and I told her to cook some *ine*, and she did not seem to know what I meant."

"*Ine* means only that rice which is growing in the rice paddies. It is rice that grows."

"I see," replied Linda writing busily in her notebook. "Then I will say to the maid go and buy me some *ine.*"

Ito San bowed low. "Forgive me, O Honorable Mistress, the rice in the shop is not called *ine* for that is the rice of the fields. The rice in the shop is called by the name of rice that has not yet been cooked in the pot. It is called *kome!*"

With despair, Linda memorized the word for uncooked rice. And then she dared to ask the little interpreter what she should say to her patient when it was time to eat rice.

She was amazed when Ito San asked her with more bows whether the patient was a child or a grown person.

"What difference could that make?" By now Linda was completely confused.

"One speaks with less courtesy to a child, and so the rice that a child eats is called *mama.*"

"And the rice which you serve to a grownup is called by a different name?"

"Yes, Honorable One from Over-the-Seas, in offering a dish of rice to a grown person, one offers it with great courtesy, calling the rice by a courteous name."

"By what name?" asked Linda wearily.

"In speaking to another person about the eating of rice, one says with a bow that one is humbly offering the other one a dish of *gozen.*"

"Then a child eats *mama,* a grown person eats *gozen,*" Linda repeated the two words with despair.

Ito San bowed again to the floor. "Let me be humble to correct, O Honored Mistress. Only the other person eats *gozen*. But when the person himself eats rice, he does not honor himself so much. He calls his rice more humbly by the plainer name of *meshi*."

Linda closed the notebook. She did not want the little interpreter to see how discouraged she felt. She clapped her hands, and the maid of the Mission House appeared with a *hibachi,* in which there were two gleaming embers of charcoal.

Then the maid glided out and returned with the *chadogu,* the hot water, the tray, the tiny teapot, the canister, the cups without handles and the other articles necessary for making tea.

Linda made the tea, first cooling the water below the boiling point, so as not to take too much of the strength at the first drawing; then she passed the tiny cup to Ito San, who received it with a deep bow.

After the tea drinking the lesson continued. "In America," she told Ito San, "for those who have been very sick, we prepare a strengthening drink made from the juice boiled from meat."

She was proud that she had learned the word for meat, *neko,* which she said over several times. She could not understand why Ito San looked so horrified.

"O Honored Mistress," the little interpreter finally begged, "please do not speak of boiling what some of the Buddhist believers might think to be the transmigrated soul of one of their ancestors."

"The soul of an ancestor?" Linda did not understand in the slightest what the distressed Ito San was trying to say.

At lengh Ito San explained. "A transmigrated soul, the Buddhists believe, may often come to live in the body of an honored cat."

"Cat?" cried Linda. "Who is speaking of cats?"

"O Honored One, did you not say quite distinctly that to help the sick ones beyond the seas, you give them the juice of boiled cat, *neko?*"

Linda could not help laughing. "We do not boil cats in our country," she said. "We pet them, just as you do here. What we boil is the meat of a cow."

"Oh, then, most Honorable One, the word to say is *niku,* cow, and not *neko,* cat."

The lesson went on, hour after hour. Late in the night Linda lay awake murmuring over and over again the nine different words for the one word, *rice;* the complicated expressions for saying good morning, and farewell, *sayonara.*

Several days later she faced her first class in nursing. The five young women in kimonos knelt before her with writing brushes in their hands. Ito San knelt close beside the teacher, who also knelt, but under her knees she had a cushion.

Linda was about to start the first lesson as she

always began the instruction for nurses—with directions in the art of taking care of a bed patient.

She suddenly corrected herself. "We shall speak today about preparing a mat on the floor, so that the sick person may be comfortable when the nurse takes care of him."

Linda spoke and Ito San's gentle singsong droned on. The girls bent over their writing brushes, making queer signs on the thin rice paper spread out before them. And so began the first instruction of nurses in Japan.

Chapter XV

Ito San came to call Linda. "A patient has come to the hospital!"

Linda went downstairs to the dispensary where Dr. Berry was patiently greeting two Japanese women in fine silken robes who kept bowing to the floor. The younger woman had a tiny baby tied to her back.

The older woman, evidently the grandmother of the infant, explained the malady of the child in the usual roundabout way. "He is the son of my son, the first-born in the house. And as you can see, O Honorable Bearded One, the child was born with sore eyes."

She explained that since this was the first-born son of her son's household, that she, the grandmother, had sought every kind of cure. The eyelids of the child had been rubbed with dust from the sacred images in the temple. A scrap of paper written with holy writing had been pasted to his forehead. The Japanese doctor had come in his ceremonial robes, a messenger running before him with the polished cabinet holding many medical powders. *Mogusa* had been burnt on the baby's skin to raise a blister.

Then finally, the grandmother had gone to a sorceress to ask her to spin the disease compass, in order to tell the baby's relatives in which direction they should go to seek a cure for the heir of the household.

"The compass," said the grandmother, "pointed directly, O Honorable One, to the house of the sick of the foreign ones, and we beg you to put hands on the child to cure him!"

All this was translated to Linda by Ito San who stood near her. Finally the baby was put into Dr. Berry's hands.

It took him only an instant to lift up the swollen lids of the child and see what the trouble was. "A serious case of *ophthalmia neonatorum,*" he told Linda, "very common in this country where no care is taken of the eyes of the infant at birth."

Linda was familiar with the disease. The membrane of the eye becomes badly inflamed and purulent. If the infection reaches the cornea, the transparent anterior part of the eyeball, then the patient may be blind for life.

Dr. Berry told the grandmother and the silent mother that the baby should be left in the hospital.

"With no relative to take care of him?" They asked in great consternation.

"The nurses will be his relatives until he is well again," Dr. Berry explained.

He turned the infant over to Linda, suggesting that her probationers could help her. If the sight of the child was to be saved, the inflamed eyes had to be cleansed with medication every twenty minutes for the next twenty-four hours.

Although Linda had worked all day, she sat up all night with the sick baby in her arms, bathing its inflamed eyes every twenty minutes. She could not trust it to the probationers.

In the morning the mother and the grandmother arrived very early. The baby had not nursed all the previous day and was hungry. His tiny eyes opened, and his lips made sucking sounds.

When the grandmother heard from Ito San that the foreign lady had herself tended the baby all night, and that she had not slept for a moment, she bowed many times to the floor.

"She will worship the foreign lady," Ito San translated, "who had treated her grandson as if he were a relative, and not a stranger."

"Tell the grandmother," Linda said, "that to a nurse, all are relatives, all who suffer are like her own flesh and blood to be tended tenderly."

Then the grandmother said she would no longer believe that it was bad for women to be taught to nurse strangers. When the infant was finally cured, the grandmother left a gift of money. It was added to a fund that Dr. Berry was raising to buy a piece of land on which a hospital building would eventually be erected with funds donated from America. But first the Japanese had to buy the land.

Linda learned many strange Japanese customs. For instance, when someone fell ill in Japan it was considered a punishment for sin. Only relatives tended to those of their own blood who had fallen into this sin. Strangers were left unattended.

A young man from the country who worked in Kyoto became ill at his place of employment. The employer feared that the sick man would die and he did not want him on the premises, so he had some coolies carry him on a mat to the railway station to be shipped to his own province.

But the railroad officials would not allow the sick man to be put on the train, and he was left to die in the park of Kyoto. A jinrikisha man told the sick man about the hospital and he brought him to Dr. Berry, who treated him kindly and took care of him until he was well again. Afterward, he told everyone about the Honorable Bearded One who helped him, and the nurses who nursed him.

An old woman was brought in who was going blind because of cataracts. Dr. Berry, who was an excellent eye surgeon, decided to operate, and Linda nursed the old woman after the operation.

She told her, through Ito San, that if she wanted to recover she must not move her head, but lie absolutely still. Although the old woman was given these directions over and over again, she kept on stirring restlessly on her mat.

After further cautioning the woman, Linda went

off to give a lesson in surgical nursing to her students. The lesson was given in Linda's bedroom, because there was not an inch of space anywhere else.

She told the five young women about the eye case that she was tending. She explained the nature of the operation and told how the recovery of the patient depended upon only one thing—her ability to lie still without moving her head.

"Otherwise she will go blind!" Linda warned.

Ito San translated and the students gravely wrote everything down. Later they would be required to memorize every word and repeat to Ito San what the teacher had told them.

When the lesson was finished, Linda rose from her knees and went into the next room to look after her eye patient. Ito San went with her to translate what the sick woman had to say.

The patient was lying on her mat, but she did not turn her head. She spoke in swift Japanese to Ito San, who started to smile.

Linda wanted to know what the sick woman was saying. "She says, 'nurse, I have heard through the paper wall all that the teacher said in the other room. I heard Ito San tell it to all the students. I will lie very still after this. I did not understand that I was in so much danger of losing my eyes or that the teacher was anxious because I did not keep still upon my mat, without moving at all.'"

The work in the hospital went on with difficulty. Sometimes the patients did not understand. Sometimes the Japanese nurses found it difficult to carry out instructions because they conflicted with their own immemorial customs, like the time a man was brought in suffering with heart trouble and dropsy. His breath was labored and Dr. Berry prescribed a medication to stimulate the overtired heart and help it work better.

Ito San came to Linda. "The sick man will not take his medicine."

"Go and tell him he must do so!" Linda replied.

Ito San grew pale. "In our country," she said, "a woman does not dare to tell a man what to do. The man," she said, "is master. The woman is only a shadow!"

"Then come with me." Linda went into the room where the sick man lay gasping for breath.

Linda knelt by his mat, Ito San beside her. "Tell the sick man," Linda said, "that the doctor has ordered him to take his medicine. If he does not take his medicine he cannot get well."

Ito San repeated the message. The sick man looked at Linda. He looked at Ito San. Then, breathing heavily, he spoke.

"What is he saying?" Linda asked.

"He says that he had not understood that we were only telling him what the doctor had said. If the medicine is for him to get well, he will take the medicine."

When this patient felt better and was able to go home, he too, left a gift of money for the new hospital.

"It is proper," he said, "that women should care
for those who are sick. They do not give orders to
the men They only tell them what the doctor has
said."

Slowly the new ways began to win adherents. A
highborn lady, sick with diphtheria, sent a message
to the hospital. Will the hospital send someone to
direct her servants while she lies sick?

Linda went with Ito San to visit the sick woman.
She lay on a mat spread with silken coverings. Her
servants hovered anxiously about her.

"Will your nurse tell my servants what to do?"
she asked through Ito San.

"A nurse will take care of you herself, and she
will help you to get well," Ito San explained.

A probationer from the hospital was sent to tend
the sick woman day and night. Every day Linda
came with Ito San to supervise the care of the young
woman. Finally the highborn lady was well enough
to rise from her mat. She received Linda and Ito
San one day for the tea-drinking ceremony.

"It is right," she told Linda, "that in Kyoto we
should have such a hospital as it is the wish of Dr.
Berry to build. I was taught as a child never to sleep
with my head to the north, as that is for the dead,
and that if a doorway were to be built on the south-
west side of a house, it would be a door to let in
sickness."

The lady then told Linda that she did not want
to believe in these old superstitions any longer, that
she wanted to study the new ways brought by the

strangers from over the seas, who had kindly helped her to return to health. She also gave a large gift to help buy the land on which the new hospital was to be built.

Dr. Berry, who had been working as a medical missionary since 1872, had done much to help the sick in Japan. In Kobe he had founded the first prefectural, that is, the first officially approved native hospital in a prefectural district. He had served in Okayama as an adviser on the native board of health, and founded dispensaries to be operated by medical missionaries. Most important of all, he tried to teach young Japanese students the new, more exact methods of studying the human body. For the first time into Japan he introduced the teaching of anatomy by dissection.

He had done all this, and yet, during the past year, with the help of several Japanese physicians who returned from their studies in America, he treated over three thousand outpatients in the dispensary.

The frail young Japanese pioneer Joseph Neesima, who was the founder and president of Doshisha University, wrote a letter to Dr. Berry telling him, "We are glad to state that the governor and most of the well-known and leading physicians of Kyoto are contributing to the hospital fund."

Because of this interest the Kyoto Health Association was founded. Linda went to the opening ceremonies and heard many of the speakers plead for funds to build a hospital on the grounds of

Doshisha University, where it was hoped that a medical school would be founded someday.

She listened to Dr. Berry who spoke eloquently in the native tongue. Ito San, sitting beside Linda translated, what she herself could not catch.

Dr. Berry described the old way of nursing in Japan.

"An old woman, ignorant and with no special skills, hence hired cheaply, is employed. She seeks bribes from the patient. She gives him food that is forbidden. If a stimulant is prescribed for the patient, she will drink it herself, filling up the medicine bottle with water.

"She often smokes or takes opium in the sickroom, and sleeps when she is needed. She can neither read nor write. Often, too, she suggests to the wife or mother a remedy 'just as good' which helped Mrs. So and So!

"How frequently," Dr. Berry continued, "have I entered the sickroom, where strict quiet has been ordered, to find it filled with relatives and neighbors. Some are smoking, others praying aloud to the gods for the sick man's recovery; while, with doors and windows closed, candles, charcoal braziers and incense are burning up the oxygen so necessary to the patient's life, a state of things to make a strong man sick."

A letter was read from a samurai, who had been cured at the hospital. He said he was selling his home in a faraway province, to come and live near the new hospital building when it was erected. "I am getting old," he said, "and am not strong, and I shall feel easier to be near the hospital where I have received so much help!"

One Japanese gentleman rose, and then another and another. "I will give." "And I!" said another. "And I!" echoed a third.

At last the happy day came when Dr. Berry told Linda that the land for the hospital had been purchased. Workmen were engaged to put up two wooden buildings, each with piazzas for sunning.

One would be the hospital building itself, which would hold thirty patients and their relatives. In Japan a patient does not like to come to the hospital alone. "He brings with him a relative or friend," Linda wrote, "who remains throughout the illness and must be provided with a small room opening upon that of the patient."

The other building would provide bedrooms for twenty student nurses. Will there ever be that many? Linda wondered.

She sent to America for blue-striped gingham and white muslin. She herself cut out and sewed the uniforms for her five student nurses.

Linda wrote to a friend in America, "These women look very sweet in their foreign uniforms, a striped gingham dress, a white apron with a bib and a white muslin cap."

But Linda found that she had to allow her nurses to follow the Japanese custom of wearing straw sandals which could be left at the door. Very nimbly the nurses moved about over the polished floors in their white foot coverings which looked like mittens, the big toe being separated, much like a thumb, from the rest of the foot.

"It is very amusing," Linda wrote, "to see how quickly the nurses take off these foreign uniforms when off duty, and exchange them for the Japanese dress in which they can sit upon the floor and lounge with ease."

The new buildings went up quickly. They were lightly constructed, not at all like American or English buildings. But they had a roof of beautifully colored tile, and the thick walls which surrounded the hospital grounds were also covered with decorative tile.

The furniture of the hospital was very simple. "A Japanese carpenter made the beds," she wrote, "which are simply a framework of wood, with canvas stretched across to take the place of springs." And Linda described the mattresses as "a pair of thick comforters made to fit the bed. The small pillows are filled with the outer shucks of wheat.

"The nurses following the national custom, will sleep on the floor, and to keep their elaborate lacquered hairdress from being disarranged, they will sleep on a wooden headrest."

In the autumn of 1887, the season when the teahouses near the river are filled with parties of Japanese who came to view the beauties of the maple trees; on the grounds of Doshisha University, the new Doshisha Hospital and Home for Trained

Nurses drew an audience of its own. The new buildings were to be dedicated.

According to the national custom of Japan, the buildings had been decorated with flowers. In the wards, there were bouquets at every bed. Over the main entrance to the hospital a beautiful green arch had been erected into which flowering plants had been woven.

At the side of one of the buildings where a large wisteria vine had been transplanted, the green branches, not blossoming at this time of the year, had been decorated during the night with dozens of huge chrysanthemums.

Three thousand people came to view the hospital where the sick would sleep, high off the ground "on shelves placed on stilts," and where "people will hang by the hips from strange frames," for in this way beds and chairs were described.

The chief official of the Kyoto Prefecture, the Honorable Governor Kitagaki himself, came to make the speech of dedication. It was a day of triumph for Dr. Berry and he humbly told Linda so.

The following summer the first nurses were graduated. One of the young women whom Linda had trained became ill with tuberculosis and was not able to finish her work. For the other four, a great ceremony was held in the assembly room of the nurses' home.

There was an opening prayer and then speeches, followed by the awarding of diplomas. The four young women, dressed in their white uniforms, rose and came forward three steps, bowing low and holding their new diplomas to their foreheads. Then they went back four steps and again bowed low. Finally, they solemnly took their places in the front row of the audience—the first trained nurses to be graduated in Japan.

After the graduation, Ito San came to her teacher whom she loved. She told Linda that a great happiness had come for her on her day of graduation. Her husband had written to ask her to marry him again.

"He has been converted to the Western ways and is willing that I should go out to do what I have been trained to do. I may continue to nurse strangers."

Linda attended Ito San's wedding. Many years later she wrote of this occasion. "Bride and bridegroom were of the upper middle class, and I shall never forget the charming sight of the twenty women guests, all save one (myself) in flowing robes of dove-colored crepe with white silk linings. On the sleeves and on the back between the shoulders was the family crest embroidered in white silk."

The marriage feast was served in many courses and took many long hours. A number of ceremonial speeches were given. It was midnight before Ito San, standing beside her husband, said farewell to her beloved teacher. The tiny Japanese wife had tears in her eyes as she said to Linda, "I shall never forget that you have been like a mother to me."

The next year at the training school, Linda sadly missed Ito San, for she had been almost like a sister. But Linda was now able to converse in Japanese. She trained a class of over twenty students, and went out to teach home nursing to mothers and grandmothers. She was received with great civility into the homes of the highborn Japanese. The work of nursing began to spread very rapidly. In a short time, training schools were started in neighboring cities by Linda's graduates.

The five years of Linda's contract passed by so quickly that she could hardly believe that she had been in Japan so long, or that the work she had started in such a small way had flowered so quickly.

At length the time came when, like all missionaries, she had to go home. For some time she had suffered with an ear infection, and Dr. Berry felt that it could be cured only by a change of climate. Much as she would have liked to stay on in Japan, she decided to return to America.

With tears in her eyes, she said farewell to the many Japanese nurses of whom she had grown so fond. The patients whom she had treated came to bring her gifts in the assembly room at the nurses home.

"Sayonara," they whispered, bowing low to her. "Sayonara," the beautiful Japanese word of farewell echoed in her ears still, as the steamer left Yokohama, the port to which she had come so long ago with fear, a stranger in a strange land.

From the deck of the vessel, as it sailed from

Japan, she looked out for the last time at the white peak of Fujiyama, swimming in the clouds.

"Sayonara," she whispered, as there vanished into the sky last glimpse of the "honorable mountain" of Japan.

Chapter XVI

A year later, carrying a small leather bag in her hand, Linda entered the doorway of a shabby Philadelphia tenement.

She climbed one dark flight of stairs and then another. Finally in the attic, where the dreary sound of the October rain could be heard on the roof, she knocked at a door.

"What do you want?" the voice of an old woman answered crossly.

Linda pushed open the door and saw a toothless old woman on an iron bedstead. Near the bed stood a pair of crutches. The woman scowled.

"Who are you?"

"I am a visiting nurse," said Linda, looking for a place in the litter on which she might put her bag. "I have come to help you."

"I don't need any help," the old woman insisted.

"The druggist on the corner told me about your broken hip, and the varicose ulcer on your leg, which should be very hard to dress if you cannot bend," Linda explained.

"What does he mean talking about me?" the old woman flared.

"He did not talk about you." Linda cleared off the rickety chair which stood by the bed, and opening her bag, she spread out a fresh towel.

"I came to ask him if he would help me find somebody that I could nurse."

"What do you want to do that for?"

"That's my work." Linda took out a bottle of disinfectant, a dressing, some bandages and a small, shining scissors which she placed on the towel.

"Are you paid?" The old eye under drooping lids regarded Linda with a shrewdly appraising look.

"Yes."

"Who pays you?"

"The Philadelphia Visiting Nurses Society."

"And if you don't find anybody to nurse, then you won't get paid?"

"Quite possibly not."

"Well," the old woman thrust out her badly discolored leg on which there was tied a filthy, dried bandage, "in that case I will help you. I will let you bandage my leg."

Linda put on a fresh dressing over the deep varicose ulcer. She tidied the bed. She warmed water and washed the old woman. She prepared her some food and fed her. A little color came into the wrinkled cheeks. The fierce expression in the old eyes softened. "If you want to," she said, "you may come back tomorrow."

Linda went out into the street again. The rain had stopped. She went from one tenement building to another. In one dim flat she showed a mother how to make a steam tent for her baby who was sick with croup. In another flat she told a grandmother that she would send someone to fumigate the bedroom where her grandchild had lain sick with diphtheria.

She stopped in some basement rooms where the father of the family had long been sick with consumption. Although she had long been trying to teach this family the meaning of germs, she found the father feeding his little girl from his own dish and with his own spoon.

Linda spoke patiently to the wife. "Your husband is sick because of germs so tiny you cannot see them."

"Did anyone ever see them?" asked the wife.

"Yes, with a special kind of magnifying glass they can be seen. I have seen them. There are millions of them crawling round on that spoon from which your little girl has been eating. If you feed her from the same dishes as your husband, she will fall ill with the same sickness. And then you will have two sick people on your hands."

"I will boil the dishes," promised the wife.

As Linda went out into the street again to wait for the horsecar which would take her to her office on the other side of the city, she saw a little girl playing near a puddle of muddy water.

She noticed that the child kept rubbing her eyes, which were red and very badly inflamed. She went up to the child.

"Will you take me to see your mother?"

She followed the little girl through a littered alley to a steamy kitchen hung with clotheslines, where a thin, bony woman bent over a tub filled with dirty clothes.

"How long has your little girl been suffering with those inflamed eyes?" Linda asked.

"Oh, a long time," the mother replied. "I keep sending to the drugstore for medicines, but they just don't do her any good. She keeps on rubbing them and I think that's what makes 'em worse."

Linda explained the nature of ophthalmia, a dangerous eye infection which might make the child blind, if she were not treated promptly.

"Leave your washing right now and take the child immediately to the dispensary, where the doctor will take care of her without charging you. If a nurse is needed, I will send someone to help you!"

"What about the medicines?" the woman asked.

"You shall have those without charge also."

Linda returned to the office of the Philadelphia Visiting Nurses Society on Race Street, where for a year she had been in charge of four visiting nurses, two of these pupil nurses.

171

On returning from Japan a year ago, Linda had not gone back to the work in which she had pioneered for ten years, that of training hospital nurses.

All over the country, hospitals had started schools to train nurses. In the last decade more than thirty fine schools had been established.

Alice Fisher, a Nightingale nurse, had given her life to start a training school for nurses at old Blockley in Philadelphia. Beautiful Isabel Hampton was pioneering in a new kind of nursing education with higher standards at Johns Hopkins Hospital in Baltimore.

But one need of the sick had long been neglected, that of the chronically ill, the aged, the disabled; that of mothers confined, and of sickly children ill at home, in want of nursing care.

This need had been visualized in England by a man of great heart who could feel the needs of others as keenly as he had felt his own personal tragedy.

He was William Rathbone VI, a member of the famous family of Liverpool philanthropists who were related to the Nightingales, and who long had worked for the better care of the sick.

When Mr. Rathbone's wife lay dying she had been cared for by Mary Robinson, an excellent trained nurse. When his wife passed away, Mr. Rathbone thought with compassion of the many poor sick people who had no nurses to help them.

172

He engaged Mary Robinson to go out and nurse in one poor family after another. When she could no longer do this work, he set up a special school at the Royal Infirmary in Liverpool to train nurses for such work among the poor. Since each nurse was assigned to work in a separate district, these nurses were called district nurses. The work spread to all cities in England.

In 1828, a Quaker physician Dr. Joseph Warrington had trained women in midwifery at his home, and sent them out to nurse mothers and babies needing help.

In Boston, a group of women had started an office from which they sent out nurses to take care of the sick and aged in their homes. And in Buffalo, a similar group was being started.

Mrs. Brooks Herford, an Englishwoman who happened to be a member of the District Nursing Committee in Manchester, came to America to visit with her friend Mrs. William Furness Jenks, who lived near Philadelphia.

Mrs. Herford told Mrs. Jenks about the way district nursing was meeting the need among the poor sick people of England.

"I could not put from my mind," Mrs. Jenks wrote sometime later, "this wonderful idea!"

So she gathered together a group of women in her home to plan a nursing service. Each contributed a sum of money and they rented a little room on Race Street for an office. They put in an old table and a few chairs, and they bought a bale of oakum from which to make dressings. In 1886, the Philadelphia Visiting Nurses Society opened its doors.

The women themselves went from door to door in the slum areas, letting the poor people know that the nursing services were available without charge to those who could not pay. During the first year, the nurses employed by the society took care of some three hundred cases.

When Linda returned to America from Japan, she received a letter from Mrs. Jenks asking if America's first trained nurse would not pioneer in a new field. "It is our wish," wrote Mrs. Jenks, "not only to serve the indigent sick in their homes, but to train pupil nurses for this task."

In the spring of 1891, Linda took over the task of head nurse in the little office on Race Street. At the age of fifty she started a new work. All summer long and then through the autumn, Linda went from house to house in the slums near the river, handling new cases herself. In the evenings, she received reports from the two assistant nurses, and she gave instructions to her two pupils.

One evening as she sat at her desk writing a report on the cases she had seen that day, she heard the two trained nurses speaking as they came up the stairs. One said in tones of disgust, "Those people! That man I had to take care of today was filthy. He was covered with dirt from head to foot. I don't believe he ever had a bath in his life. It's enough to make a person sick!"

"I see plenty, too, every day," the other one agreed, her voice full of scorn. "I don't understand how people can be so disgusting, how they can live that way!"

Linda said nothing when the two women, both capable and experienced nurses, came in to write notes on the cases they had visited that day. Soon afterward, the two pupil nurses arrived. Linda prepared to give her nursing lessons, and she asked the two older women if they would not stay.

"When I worked in Japan," she said, "and I could not speak the language of the people, I learned that we always speak to people not only with words but with our feelings.

"A nurse should know how to do her work. And she should do her work with nicety. But still it seems to me that something more than knowledge, skill and efficiency is involved when we deal in the most intimate way with human beings entrusted to our care.

"They sense our feelings and are affected by our feelings. The most skillful nurse in the world can still be a tyrant, or an offensive person. The patient is at the mercy of the one who tends him.

"Is it done compassionately, with tender feeling, or with a cold, mechanical efficiency; or, worse still, with a feeling of disgust and snobbishness toward the one who is sick?"

Linda sat holding a pencil in her hand, her head bent over the table. She was aware of the embarrassed faces of the two older nurses who had spoken with such coldness of their patients.

"In Japan they tell a story," Linda went on, "of the Buddha who washed the feet of a leper whom everyone shunned. And as the story is told, it is said that the Buddha smiled with happiness as he tended to the sick woman whom everyone loathed.

"It may be," she went on, "that such a happening never took place, that this story simply tells a truth that the people of Japan are trying to speak, that people all over the world are each trying to say in their own way."

She paused and looked around the room. The two women who had spoken sharply sat with bowed heads. Linda gathered up her papers. "It is not hard to teach nurses to do their work properly with their hands, to take temperatures, put on fomentations and make out accurate records."

She rose with a sigh, "But how can we teach nurses to have the right feelings in the heart, to help the patient by feeling for him as a human being; not to feel superior because she knows something that he has not had the good fortune to learn; or because his language or his ways are different from hers?

"How do I know all this? Because I have failed many times, and I suppose as long as I go on nursing I shall continue to fail, since nursing with the hands means so much less than nursing with the heart."

The four women left the room. Linda sat at the table for a long time before she turned out the gas lamp. How were women to be chosen for nursing, she wondered, so they would be more than professionals, so they would be women with the right feeling? To this question, not even Florence Nightingale had found the right answer.

Chapter XVII

On a spring day in 1905, a tall, gaunt woman with white hair, dressed in the starched uniform of a graduate nurse, passed on a trip of inspection through the long wards of one of America's oldest hospitals for the mentally ill.

At one of the beds she stopped to watch a young nursing probationer in a striped dress and white apron, who was struggling to free her arm held firmly by a young man with tragic dark eyes who did not seem to want to let her go.

"What is the trouble here?" Linda asked of the young girl, whose face had flushed with the struggle. The patient let go instantly. The probationer snapped to attention before her superintendent.

For six years now Linda Richards had been engaged in the pioneering work of training nurses to take care of the mentally ill. She had started a training school at the Massachusetts mental hospital in Taunton, and now she had come to start such a school at the Worcester State Hospital.

"I just can't get my work done," the young

probationer complained. "Whenever I have to go by Jimmy's bed here, he reaches out and grabs my arm, and then he won't let me go!"

Linda looked down at the thin young man who sat on the bed, rubbing his hands together with an expression of abject misery. She sat down beside him and put her arm around his shoulder.

"Do you like your nurse very much?" she asked.

He nodded his head mutely. His eyes filled with tears. "Is that why you pull at her arm, because you want her to sit down for a little while beside you?" Once more he nodded. Linda patted his shoulder. "You have been talking to your nurse, haven't you Jimmy, quite in your own way? You have been telling her, haven't you, that you feel lonesome, and you want her to visit with you now and then when she goes by through the ward?

"Well, Jimmy, I think she feels quite complimented that you want her to be your friend." The patient stopped rubbing his hands together nervously. He clasped Linda's arm now, wrinkling the stiffly starched cuff. She did not loosen his fingers, but let him hold onto her, with her other hand softly stroking his shoulders. After a moment, with a sigh of contentment he let her go.

Later that day, Linda called the young probationer into her office. The young woman fearing a reprimand stood nervously at attention.

Linda smiled warmly. "Sit down, Jane," she

said. "I would like to ask you a question. Why have you taken up the study of nursing?"

The girl sank down into the armchair which stood facing Linda's desk, and pressing her hands together said in a low voice, "I really want to help people."

"Good," Linda assured her, "and you have chosen a work where you can help the loneliest and the most neglected people in the whole world. We all understand physical suffering. If a man is hurt in an accident, or is brought into a hospital moaning with pain, the doctors and nurses hurry to help him. The members of his family feel the deepest anguish for his agony."

"Of course," said the girl.

"But if that same man should be hurt, not in his body but in his mind, if he suffers not physical pain but mental torment, do we feel the same concern, are we as sympathetic?"

"But . . ." the girl began.

Linda stopped her. "You may think the mentally sick have no feelings. They feel far more than you or I. They feel unwanted, unloved, and they desperately need love."

The girl rose. She stood silent for a moment. "Then Jimmy pulled on my arm, not to annoy me, not to be mean?"

"Of course not. He wanted to know that you remembered him, that you felt for him as a human being!"

Linda stood in the doorway watching the young

nurse as she went down the hall. A dozen years ago, Linda's interest in the mentally ill had been stirred.

She had left her work with the Philadelphia Visiting Nurses Society, because the need to be out in all kinds of weather had brought on a renewal of her ear trouble. And taking a post as matron at the Kirkbride Hospital for the Insane she saw what she had never been able to neglect—a great need!

In the splendid hospital, known as a model institution architecturally, she found what she had once seen at the Massachusetts General Hospital, immaculate wards and neglected patients.

The attendants hired to care for the sick were ignorant, uncouth, poorly paid, chosen from the very dregs of the city's population.

She went before the board of trustees. "It stands to reason," she urged, "that the mentally sick should be at least as well cared for as the physically sick!" And she offered to set up a training school in the hospital to train nurses for the special care of the mentally sick patients.

The board members laughed at Linda. The patients would not know the difference, they insisted, no matter who cared for them.

For several months, Linda tried to convince the board members. Then, discouraged, she left her post at Kirkbride. She spent the next half a dozen years at her old work, as a director of training in general hospitals. She went from hospital to hospital, improving courses and lengthening the period of training.

She served as matron and superintendent of training at the Methodist Episcopal Hospital in Philadelphia, at the Brooklyn Homeopathic Hospital, at the Hartford Hospital, at the University of Pennsylvania Hospital. She returned to serve for a year at her alma mater, the New England Hospital for Women and Children, where she had received her diploma as America's first trained nurse.

In hundreds of nursing schools modeled after those she had first founded, over four thousand nurses were receiving their diplomas each year!

New fields had opened in nursing. The first factory nurse had been employed, and the first school nurse. And in a tenement flat in New York, a great nurse Lillian Wald had opened up the new career of public health nursing.

But the needs of the mentally ill remained neglected. Linda wrote to one mental institution after another, offering her services as director of a school to train psychiatric nurses. She received cold replies.

"It must be," she confided to a friend, "that the time is not ripe!"

The Spanish-American War broke out. Young men flocked to follow Theodore Roosevelt and his Rough Riders avenging the sinking of the *Maine* with a charge on San Juan Hill in Cuba. Nurses of distinction organized nursing corps to serve the troops. The newspapers wrote about these heroines of nursing.

Linda was not among those honored. Hardly aware that a war existed, she carried on all alone the battle to stir compassion for the mentally ill.

Finally, from a bleak little town in southern Massachusetts, where the grim towers of an asylum overlooked the flat landscape, she received an offer which she eagerly accepted.

In September, 1899, she arrived in Taunton, where she had grudgingly been given the opportunity "to train female attendants" at the Taunton Hospital for the Insane.

She organized a three-year training course, with two years of training to be given at the mental institution, and one year at a nearby general hospital, so that when they graduated the nurses would be fitted for every kind of duty.

She searched for students. She won over parents. She lured instructors in nursing to the out-of-the-way town. She cajoled, threatened, raged and inspired. In 1904, the first class of psychiatric nurses won their caps. With tears in her eyes, Linda bestowed the diplomas!

"The average probationer," she said, "may not possess much patience or tact when she starts her training. It is wonderful to see spirited young women growing in grace, as day by day they develop that sweetness of disposition and strength of character required for nursing the mentally afflicted."

All nurses might benefit by such training, Linda

thought. Too many nurses, proud of their crisp white uniforms, had lost what it takes to make a good nurse—heart!

She spoke these views at a convention of nurses in Boston, and saw from the faces of those around her that they thought her sentimental.

She went on to found a school of psychiatric nursing at the Worcester Hospital for the Insane, the oldest mental hospital in Massachusetts, founded by Horace Mann and improved by Dorothea Lynde Dix, the great fighter for the mentally ill.

On the steps of one of the old buildings, Linda's picture was snapped by one of the doctors as she sat surrounded by young women with radiant faces, all in white caps, her graduates. Under the picture she wrote, "My bouquet of humanity!"

She heard that the Kalamazoo Asylum in Michigan wanted to found a training school for psychiatric nurses, and at the age of sixty-five she undertook this pioneering effort, remaining until September, 1909, when her first class was graduated. For the last time she handed out diplomas.

Florence Nightingale had passed away. Mrs. Wardroper was gone. All of Linda's contemporaries had vanished. She returned to the East, weary and depleted.

At the first school of psychiatric nursing which she had founded in Taunton, the superintendent of nurses had resigned and a new superintendent could not be found.

With her last strength, Linda worked six months

more until she could be relieved, retiring in March, 1911, at the age of seventy and with the title of superintendent emeritus.

The moment she ceased to work, the weariness of a lifetime descended on her with a crushing weight, the years of endeavor rushed away, leaving an echoing silence.

Dazed, bewildered, without plan, for she had always planned only for others, she went to rest for a few days with some distant relatives, a young couple living in the Massachusetts village of Foxboro. She remained with them for five years.

The people of the town did not know that there lived in the little white house, not far from the main street, a woman who had once been a famous nurse.

She sat by the window whole days at a time. She saw the seasons pass. The fashions changed as the years went by. Wasp waists vanished, the Gibson girl disappeared. Young women hobbled by in long, tight skirts. People stopped to talk of distant events: armies that marched in Europe, soldiers that died in the trenches.

One day the Boston newspaper that was read in Foxboro streamed with black banners. The *Lusitania* had been sunk by German submarines. The president called for war! Twenty-five thousand nurses in blue capes and white uniforms marched down Fifth Avenue, ready to leave for the battlefields.

The old woman in Foxboro wondered if Florence Nightingale could have dreamed that so great an army could have come from the little corps of untrained women she led to Scutari!

Laying awake in the nights, as the aged often do, on occasion Linda dreamed of the old days of endeavor. Like pictures dropped, sometimes there tumbled into her mind the vanished faces of long ago.

She saw Florence Nightingale on her couch, making notes about the new ways of nursing in America. She saw Mrs. Wardroper in her cap with ribbons, writing out orders, her hands encased in black gloves.

She saw Sister Helen, waxen, impassive, at her side the silver crucifix of the Anglican nursing order. She saw Ito San, her beautiful dark head bent, kneeling at a low table, making columns of winged marks.

She saw Dr. Dimock, beautiful and calm, a cameo at her throat, taking from her desk a scroll of stiff white paper, the first diploma to be granted to a trained nurse in America.

The war in Europe, grinding out millions of lives, stopped at last. The day of the Armistice fell. People wept. Confetti fell in the streets. Everyone shouted there would never be another war!

On a November evening in 1922, there was held a celebration of the fiftieth anniversary of the opening of the New England Hospital for Women and Children in Roxbury.

Linda Richards, now a thin little old woman of

over eighty, was seated on the platform in the Surgical Building, as a long line of nurses and alumnae marched into the lecture hall. She was presented with a bouquet of fifty beautiful red roses, one rose for each year of her service to mankind. She sat overwhelmed, unable to speak.

She appeared in public for the last time a year later, at a meeting of Massachusetts nurses held in Swampscott. In a hotel by the pounding sea, on a summer day when the sound of the waves echoed through the open windows, this tiny, bent old woman in a black gown rose and looked down from the platform at the room swimming before her, the faces for a moment merging. The applause and the rhythm of the sea swept against her heart like beating waves.

Then she found her voice and began to speak. The thin, quavering voice rose in the stillness of the room, where only the echoing thud of the waves could be heard, a sound like the beating of a human heart.

"The nurse is a human being, and the patient is a human being. All your skill will not make you a nurse, if you do not have the right feeling in your heart for your patient.

"It is lonely to be sick. The nurse can help the sick person in his loneliness by being there to help, not just with the head and the hands, but with the heart."

She sat down. The silence in the room made her think that no one had heard her. Then like a sob, the applause broke out, to echo and re-echo again like the sound of the beating surf outside.

Linda returned to the little house in Foxboro. She felt very weary. One night soon afterward she suffered a stroke. The memories of her life merged strangely. She seemed to be at once both an old woman and a child.

She was moved to a nursing home in Grafton. And then the nurses in the New England Hospital for Women and Children heard of her illness and sent an ambulance to bring her home.

In the hospital from which she had been graduated, she lay ill for many, many months. She heard of scholarships named in her honor, of awards endowed with her name. She felt the passage of time through the change of the seasons as she looked at the window.

Sometimes she roused herself. One day she asked the nurse who sat by her bedside, "Are the nurses doing their work properly today?"

"Everything is being done as it should be!"

"Good," she murmured. "Well done."

On an April morning in 1930, only a few months before her ninetieth birthday, she fell asleep for the last time.

She had asked that there should be no ceremonies for her interment, that her body should be cremated. She had no relations. Who would come to her funeral? Who would remember her?

Eighteen years later, the nursing world celebrated the diamond jubilee of her graduation, and mayors in sixty-three cities and governors in forty-eight states ordered special observances of Linda Richards day!

The American Nurses Association gave Linda Richards awards that year to the outstanding nurse to be graduated in each of the forty-eight states, each winner receiving a medal engraved with the likeness of Linda Richards.

In the hospital from which she had been graduated, a memorial room was dedicated, the Linda Richards room. To this room come nurses from all over the world, to see the mementos of her life: the uniform she wore, her Bible, a handful of yellowed letters, her mother's picture—the physical objects that imprint a lifetime.

On a summer day in 1948, nurses gathered in the Forest Hills Crematory near Boston, and a wreath was placed over an urn which contained the ashes of America's first trained nurse. The wreath framed the simple inscription:

MELINDA ANN JUDSON RICHARDS

1841–1930

Suggestions for Further Reading

Andrews, Mary Raymond. *A Lost Commander: Florence Nightingale*. Garden City: Doubleday, Doran, 1929.

Baker, Rachel. *The First Woman Doctor*. New York: Julian Messner, Inc., 1942.

Berry, Katherine Fiske. Letters and catalogues of Doshisha University from the private collection of.

———. *A Pioneer Doctor in Old Japan*. New York: Fleming H. Revell Co., 1940.

Breckenridge, Mary. *A Story of the Frontier Nursing Service*. New York: Harper & Brothers, 1952.

Cutolo, Salvatore R. *Bellevue Is My Home*. Garden City: Doubleday & Co., 1956.

De Kruif, P. H. *Men Against Death*. New York: Harcourt, Brace & Co., 1932.

Dickens, Monica. *One Pair of Feet*. New York: Harper & Brothers, 1942.

Gordon, M. L. *Thirty Eventful Years*. American Board, 1901.

Kern, C. *Nursing Through the Years*. New York: E. P. Dutton & Co., 1936.

Koch, H. R. *Militant Angel*. New York: The Macmillan Co., 1951.

Mead, K. C. *A History of Women in Medicine.* New York: Haddam Press, 1938.

Nolan, Jeannette Covert. *Florence Nightingale.* New York: Julian Messner, Inc., 1946.

Poole, Ernest. *Nurses on Horseback.* New York: The Macmillan Co., 1932.

Richards, Linda. *Reminiscences of Linda Richards.* Whitcomb & Barrows, 1911.

Robinson, Victor. *The Story of Medicine.* New York: Tudor Publishing Co.

Shippen, Katherine. *Men of Medicine.* New York: The Viking Press, Inc.

Sigerist, Henry. *Great Doctors.* Garden City: Doubleday & Co., 1958.

Sloan, Isabelle W. *America's First Trained Nurse: The Story of Linda Richards.* Boston, 1941.

Stewart, Isabel M. *The Education of Nurses.* New York: The Macmillan Co., 1943.

Victor, A. C. *A Woman's Quest: The Life of Marie Zakrzewska, M.D.* New York: Appleton-Century-Crofts, Inc., 1924.

Yost, Edna. *American Women of Nursing.* Philadelphia: J. B. Lippincott Co., 1947.

Index